Better Homes and Gardens®

——1989——
CHRISTMAS CRAFTS

Library of Congress Catalog Card Number: 89-60203
ISBN: 0-696-01796-2

*T*hroughout the
*Christmas season, families and friends
gather together to enjoy the special
activities that this holiday inspires. To
help you create your own fun and
festive traditions, we've collected our
favorite Christmas projects from*
Better Homes and Gardens® *magazine
and crafts publications and assembled
them into one book—*1989 Christmas
Crafts.

*As you leaf through these colorful
pages, you'll find lots of projects to
keep your family busy—and happy—
right through Christmas Eve, year
after year.*

Contents

Christmas in Our Town

The sparkle, richness, and elegance of Victorian style make everyone feel at home at Christmas. Our collection of Victorian-style decorations creates a wonderful holiday home and the accompanying gifts are handmade treasures that family and friends will cherish.

A Victorian custom was to decorate the Christmas tree with American flags. The magnificent tree, *left,* demonstrates this delightful tradition, and also features handmade decorations.

A cross-stitch alphabet, arranged in the shape of a Christmas tree, is used on the oval ornaments. Pretty crocheted ornaments in three different shapes add a delicate, lacy touch. Cording covered with red-and-white-striped fabric is braided into peppermint wreaths. Strips of velvet are coiled tightly into the roses on the tree and on the wreath, *right.*

Instructions begin on page 16.

Doves have been the universal symbol of peace and tranquillity for centuries, and the paper version, *above left,* is a beautiful representation of this revered bird. A plain white sheet of paper and a bit of glue are the only materials you'll need to make this trim, which you can use as a tree ornament or to accent a special package. A pierced design made with a needle provides the feather details.

Spraying walnuts and other natural materials with gold paint to make Christmas decorations is a childhood memory for many of us. The tree, *below left,* shows us how timeless these decorations can be. To make a batch of gilded walnuts, lay a couple dozen nuts in a shallow cardboard box and spray with gold paint. After the paint dries, turn the nuts over to paint another side. Continue until the nuts are coated thoroughly. Add bell caps (available at crafts supply stores) and hang with thread.

Needlework was a favorite Victorian pastime, and crochet was especially popular because of the lacy looks a crocheter could create. The three ornaments, *opposite,* combine simple shapes with lace borders, three-dimensional flowers, and lush tassels and ribbon trims.

Theorem paintings were used around the turn of the century to teach elementary painting techniques. The portraits, *left,* painted on velveteen backgrounds, are similar to those created at that time. Use stencils to duplicate the basic shapes in these portraits, and because you use slow-drying oil paints to make them, you can add shading and details until you're pleased with the results.

The same alphabet used for the tree ornaments on page 6, makes the fine sampler, *above right,* when stitched on fabric with a different stitch count. To accent this sampler, surround it with a quilted-fabric mat and wood frame. To cover the mat, pad a piece of chintz with batting; quilt around the major design elements with gold metallic thread. Baste piping around center opening; line fabric, finishing the center opening. Slip mat between the fabric and the lining.

Hunt for lovely print fabrics in red and green for the appliqué pillow, *below right.* Use machine stitching to outline each print shape, and add a generous ruffle.

You usually can find even-weave fabric squares in holiday colors at your needlework supply shop. For the initial pillow, *below right,* select a square with a plaid border, and stitch an initial or monogram in the center of it with metallic floss.

Except for their sizes, the big and little sister dolls, *above left,* are alike in every way. Use scraps of muslin to make their bodies, and style their braids from any kind of yarn or string. Only the simplest embroidery stitches are needed for their facial features. Because these dolls are dressed in their Sunday best, choose good-quality cottons or wools in tiny prints or plaids for the dresses.

The cuddly bear, *below left,* is attached to its very own base to transform it into a pull toy. For the pull toy base, attach purchased wheels to the wood rectangle, or secure wood circles to a dowel axle. Fake fur or any other fabric, trimmed with a wreath of jingle bells and a ribbon bow, makes this a classically styled teddy that can stand alone.

Dressed in eyelet finery, the rag baby doll, *right,* will be loved and cherished by both little girls and collectors. Make this doll from muslin and add sweetly embroidered eyes, nose, and mouth. Lengths of clipped embroidery floss tacked to the doll's head create silky hair. For the dress and bonnet, use embroidered eyelet fabric accented with white satin ribbons.

Ladies' gloves and children's mittens trim the miniature tree, *left.* Begin with four felt cutouts for the mitten ornaments, and embroider two of them with the flowered wreath motif. Then stitch the mitten tops to the bottoms, trim the wrist edge with lace, and glue the mittens to a hair clip for attaching them to the tree.

The gloves, which are suspended from the tree singly instead of in pairs, are constructed similarly. They have stitched lines to outline the fingers and a small beribboned bouquet at the wrist.

You often can find tattered bits and pieces of Victorian crazy quilt patchwork at antiques shops. To put them to good use, stitch them into the heart-shaped ornaments, *left.* Or, create your own antique-look fabric from satins, velvets, and taffetas.

More fabric scraps—of chintz and velvet—combine to make the stocking, *above.* The simple stocking shape is quilted with gold thread and topped with a velvet cuff trimmed with cording and bells.

Alphabet Tree Ornament and Sampler

Ornament is on page 6; sampler is on page 11.
Ornament is 3½x5¾ inches; sampler is 6x9⅜ inches.
Design is 64 stitches wide and 104 stitches high.

MATERIALS
For ornament
8x10-inch piece of white 18-count Aida cloth
Fabric for backing
Piping; polyester fiberfill

For sampler
21x24-inch piece of ecru hardanger

For both projects
DMC embroidery floss: 1 skein *each* of green (561), olive (731), deep rose (326), navy (336), and rose (335)
Embroidery hoop; tapestry needle

INSTRUCTIONS
Referring to chart, *opposite,* transfer pattern to graph paper, if desired. Or, work directly from page.

Locate center of fabrics and chart; begin stitching tree at center.

For ornament, use two plies of floss and work the cross-stitches over one thread of fabric. For sampler, use three plies of floss and work the cross-stitches over two threads of fabric.

Press fabric on the wrong side. Frame sampler as desired.

To assemble ornament, mark an oval on right side of fabric. Cut out, adding ¼-inch seam allowances. Cut a backing to match. Stitch piping to front oval along outline. For ruffle, cut a 2½-inch-wide strip of fabric that is twice as long as the perimeter of the oval; fold lengthwise, wrong sides facing, and gather to fit around oval outline. Stitch to front at piping line. Place right sides of front and back together; stitch around, leaving an opening for turning. Clip curves, turn, press, stuff, and close.

Peppermint Wreaths
Shown on page 6.
Finished diameter is 5 inches.

MATERIALS
For eight wreaths
1¼ yards of 45-inch-wide red-and-white-striped fabric
12 yards of ½-inch-diameter cable cord
1½ yards of piping cord

INSTRUCTIONS
Cut fabric into 2-inch-wide bias strips.

Cut 48-inch lengths of cable cord and fabric strips. Overlap end of piping cord to end of cable cord about 1 inch; sew together securely.

To cover cable cord with fabric, fold fabric in half lengthwise over piping, right sides together. Sew ¼ inch from raw edge and across end where piping joins cable cord; leave tube open at other end.

Gently pull out piping from fabric, turning fabric right side out and over cable cord. Using the same piece of piping, repeat seven more times.

Cut cord into 15-inch lengths. Pull cord ¼ inch from each end; trim. Turn under and baste raw edges.

Twist two lengths together evenly, matching ends to form circle. Sew ends together. Loosely wrap third length in opposite direction; sew ends together. Trim with bow.

Velvet Roses
Shown on page 7.

MATERIALS
6-inch strips of 45-inch-wide velvet
Silk leaf clusters (available at florist's supply stores)
Florist's wire; gold spray paint

INSTRUCTIONS
Tie 12-inch length of wire to center of velvet strip. Attach wire to back of chair or stair rail for support while making rose.

Beginning at point where wire is tied and working toward ends of velvet strip, twist ends of velvet tightly in opposite directions, caus-ing fabric to curl for flower center. Refer to photograph, page 7.

Working with the natural curl, continue twisting ends around center, overlapping or intertwining as necessary to hold.

Bring ends to back of rose. Remove from support; wire ends.

Spray leaf clusters gold. Attach to back of rose; shape as desired.

Secure with remaining wire.

Crocheted Ornaments
Shown on pages 6 and 9.

MATERIALS
DMC Cébélia, Size 10
Size 8 steel crochet hook
¼-inch-wide satin ribbon
Polyester fiberfill

Abbreviations: See page 84.

INSTRUCTIONS
Note: There are three ornaments: Round, Square, and Cylinder.

For the round ornament
Ch 8, join with sl st to form ring.
Rnd 1: Work 16 sc in ring; join.
Rnd 2: Ch 3, dc in same st; * dc in next sc, 2 dc in next sc; rep from *—24 dc; join to top of beg ch-3.
Rnd 3: Ch 3, dc in same st; * dc in next 2 dc, 2 dc in next dc, rep from * around—32 dc; join.
Rnd 4: Ch 3, dc in same st, * dc in next dc, 2 dc in next dc, rep from * around—48 dc; join.
Rnd 5: Ch 3, dc in same sp, * dc in next 2 dc, 2 dc in next dc, rep from * around—64 dc; join.
Rnd 6: Repeat Rnd 4—96 dc.
Rnd 7: Work as before, having 5 dc between incs—112 dc. Break off thread. Begin a second motif.
Rnd 2: Ch 3, in same st work dc, ch 2, and 2 dc; * sk 3 sc, in next sc make 2 dc, ch 2, and 2 dc—shell made; rep from * around; join to top of ch-3.

FINISHING: Lay medallions wrong sides together with a medallion attached to ball of thread on top. Work 1 rnd sc around through double thickness on 100 sts. Stuff
continued

ALPHABET TREE ORNAMENTS

COLOR KEY

◨	Deep Rose (326)	●	Navy Blue (336)
⊡	Rose (335)	⊠	Dark Sea Foam Green (561)
		⊞	Dark Olive Green (731)

medallion; work last 12 sc through double thickness to close; join.

Rnd 3: Sl st to ch-2 center of first shell; ch 3, in same st work dc, **ch 4, sl st in third ch from hook—picot made;** ch 1, and 2 dc; * in ch-2 sp of next shell work 2 dc, ch 4, make picot, ch 1, and 2 dc; rep from * around; join. End off.

FLOWER: Ch 8, join with sl st.
Rnd 1: Work 16 sc in ring; join.
Rnd 2: Ch 5, * sk sc, dc in next sc, ch 2; rep from * around; join in third ch of beg ch-5—8 spokes.
Rnd 3: Sl st into first sp, ch 1, in same sp work sc, 3 hdc, and sc; ch 1, * in next sp work **sc, 3 hdc, and sc—petal made;** ch 1; rep from * around; join to beg ch.
Rnd 4: (Ch 4, holding petal forward, sc bet next 2 petals) 8 times; end ch 4, join with sc in first ch-4 lp.
Rnd 5: In same lp, work hdc, 3 dc, hdc, and sc; * ch 1, in next lp work sc, hdc, 3 dc, hdc, and sc; rep from * around; join in sc at beg of Rnd 4.
Rnd 6: Rep Rnd 4, making ch-5 lps instead of ch-4 lps; join with sc in first ch-5 lp.
Rnd 7: Work sc, hdc, 2 dc, trc, 2 dc, hdc, and sc in each ch-5 lp around. Fasten off.

For the square ornament
Ch 8, join with sl st to form ring.
Rnd 1: Work 16 sc in ring; join.
Rnd 2: Ch 3, in same st work dc, ch 2, and 2 dc; * dc in each of next 3 sc, in next st work 2 dc, ch 2, and 2 dc; rep from * around—four corner shells; join.
Rnd 3: Sl st to corner ch-2 sp, ch 3; in same sp work dc, ch 2, and 2 dc; dc in next 7 dc, * in next ch-2 corner sp work 2 dc, ch 2, and 2 dc; dc in next 7 dc; rep from * around; join.
Rnds 4–8: Rep Rnd 3, having 4 more dc on each side every rnd.
Break thread. Work second motif but do not break thread. Lay motifs wrong sides together. Line up corners and sides stitch for stitch. Sc around edges, working through both motifs; work 2 sc, ch 2, and 2 sc into each corner. Work around three sides and half of the fourth. Stuff medallion and complete remaining side. Do not fasten off.

BORDER: *Rnd 1:* Sl st to corner ch-2 sp; ch 3, in same sp work dc, ch 2, and 2 dc; * sk 3 sc; in next st work **2 dc, ch 2, and 2 dc—shell made;** rep from * putting a shell in each corner; join to beg ch-3 and sl st to ch-2 sp in beg corner shell.
Rnd 2: Ch 3, in same sp work dc, **ch 4, sl st in 3rd ch from hook—picot made;** ch 1, and 2 dc. In each ch-2 shell sp around work 2 dc, picot, ch 1, and 2 dc; join to top of beg ch-3. Break off thread and weave in end.

FLOWER: Ch 10, join to form ring.
Rnd 1: Work 24 sc in ring; join.
Rnd 2: Ch 3, work dc in each sc around—24 dc; join.
Rnd 3: Ch 2, * **work 7 dc into next st; drop lp from hook, insert hook into top of the first dc, and pull the dropped lp through and tighten—bobble made;** ch 2, sk next st; rep from * around—12 bobbles; join to base of beg ch-2.
Rnd 4: Sl st to center of first ch-2 sp, * ch 3, sc into next ch-2 lp; rep from * around; end ch 3, join with sl st to base of beg ch-3—12 ch-3 sps.
Rnd 5: Ch 4, in same sp work 2 trc, 2 dc, hdc, and sc; * in next ch-3 sp work sc, hdc, 2 dc, and 3 trc; in next ch-3 sp work 3 trc, 2 dc, hdc, and sc; rep from *—6 petals. End off.

For the cylindrical ornament
Ch 4, join with sl st to form ring.
Rnd 1: Work 8 sc in ring; join.
Rnd 2: 2 sc in each sc—16 sc.
Rnd 3: 2 sc in each sc—32 sc.
Rnds 4 and 5: Work sc in each sc around.
Rnd 6: Ch 1, work hdc into each sc around, through back lp only; join.
Rnds 7–32: Ch 1, work hdc in 32 hdc, working through both lps; join each rnd with sl st at end of *each* rnd in ch-1 sp.
Rnd 33: Ch 1, sc around in back lps.
Rnd 34: Ch 1, sc in each st around through both lps.
Cut two cardboard circles the same size as the beg closed end. Insert one circle into cylinder and push to closed end; stuff. Insert second circle.
Rnd 35: **Draw up a lp in each of next 2 sc, yo, draw through the 3 lps**

on the hook—dec made; work dec around—16 sc.
Rnd 36: Rep Rnd 35 ending with 8 sc, end off leaving tail. Thread tail into needle and with running stitch through rem 8 sc draw up tightly and close rem hole. Secure.

BORDER: *Row 1:* Join thread in front lp of any ch-1; ch 3, in same sp work dc, ch 2, and 2 dc; at end of every other rnd, work * **2 dc, ch 2, 2 dc—shell made;** sk next lp; rep from * around. Do not join, but continue the shells down the spiraling beg-of-rnd line, to opposite end. Turn, sl st to the center of last shell made.
Row 2: Make a shell of 2 dc, ch 1, **ch 4, sl st into 3rd ch from hook—picot made;** ch 1, and 2 dc, into each ch-2 sp in the center of each shell. Break off and weave in end. Turn cylinder upside down and rep rows 1 and 2 of border around other end into front lps of Rnd 33, continuing down and around at halfway point to other end. Sew hanging cord in center of one end. Make or buy a tassel and sew in center of other end. Trim with bow.

FINISHING: Starch shell borders, taking care not to get rest of ornament wet. Pull out each shell to its full length and position each picot facing out. Hang each ornament up and let dry. Sew flowers to center of each ornament. Add tassels and ribbons to finished ornaments.

Paper Dove
Shown on page 8.

MATERIALS
Medium-weight white paper
Pencil; needle; scissors
White glue; crafts knife

INSTRUCTIONS
Transfer full-size patterns, *opposite,* onto wrong side of paper. Cut out all pieces; pierce with needle along dotted lines from wrong side of paper.
Fold wings along dashes, right sides together. Glue creased tab together so wings meet; let glue dry.

Crease wings, right sides together, along row of piercing closest to tab; secure with glue. Curve wing on either side of crease over finger or pencil.

Glue wing shoulders over crease on wings; let dry.

Crease underwings along piercing lines, right sides together; roll scallops over finger or pencil to shape. Glue underwings to wings; let dry.

Glue head and body centers together, leaving open along upper back and tail. Fan tail to shape.

Glue tail pieces together along straight edge. Fan scalloped edges slightly to shape.

Slip wing tab into upper back between pieces and slip tail into body between pieces; glue in place.

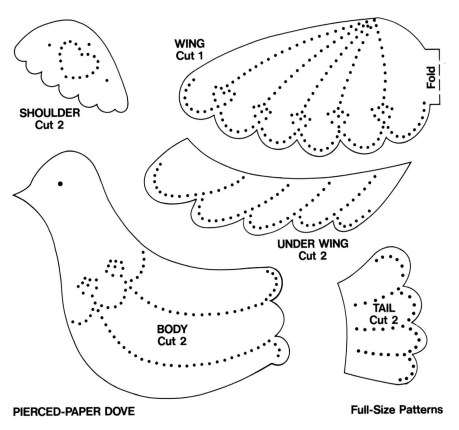

PIERCED-PAPER DOVE

SHOULDER Cut 2

WING Cut 1

Fold

UNDER WING Cut 2

TAIL Cut 2

BODY Cut 2

Full-Size Patterns

Holly Pillow

Shown on page 11.
Finished size is 14½x14½ inches.

MATERIALS

½ yard of ivory linen
1¼ yards fabric
Fabric scraps: Light burgundy, dark burgundy, olive, light green, blue-green, blue print, and blue pindot
2 yards cording
Fusible webbing; fiberfill

INSTRUCTIONS

Enlarge the pattern on page 20 and transfer to paper for master pattern. Draw a 15-inch square on linen. *Lightly* trace design onto linen.

Referring to color key, cut shapes from appropriate fabrics and fusible webbing. Omit lower branches beneath bow. Fuse pieces to linen.

Machine-zigzag-stitch around the pieces with threads matching fabrics. Zigzag-stitch lower branches; machine-stitch veins in leaves.

Cut back to match front; cover cording and baste to pillow front. For ruffle, cut and piece a 6x90-inch fabric strip; fold lengthwise with wrong sides together and press. Gather raw edges to 60 inches; stitch to front. Stitch back to front along seam line, leaving an opening. Turn, press, stuff, and close.

Initial Pillow

Shown on page 11.

MATERIALS

15x15-inch piece of 14-count Christmas even-weave fabric
Gold metallic thread
Alphabet pattern
Fabric (backing)
Piping
Embroidery hoop; tapestry needle

INSTRUCTIONS

Select letter to chart from cross-stitch pattern book; mark centers. Baste centers of fabric; bind edges with masking tape. Stitch, using sufficient thread to cover each stitch.

Steam-press on the wrong side.

Trim pillow front, allowing for ½-inch seams. Cut out a matching back; set aside. Stitch piping to pillow front along seam line, if desired.

Place front and back together, right sides facing. Stitch around, along seam line, leaving an opening for turning. Turn, stuff, and slipstitch closed.

Theorem Portraits

Shown on page 10.

MATERIALS

Two 9x12-inch pieces of off-white cotton velveteen
Oil paints in the following colors: Prussian blue, burnt umber, raw umber, yellow ochre, black, white, alizarin crimson, flesh, Indian yellow, green, and Vandyke brown
Oil and stencil brushes
Five (six for girl) sheets of 9x12-inch stencil plastic
Two 9x12-inch pieces *each* of foam-core board and cardboard
Crafts knife
Glass for cutting stencils
Spray adhesive
Paper palette or plate
Turpentine; masking tape
Palette knife or crafts stick
Fine lead pencil

continued

HOLLY APPLIQUÉ PILLOW

1 Square = 1 Inch

INSTRUCTIONS

MAKING STENCILS: Trace outlines on pages 21 and 22 for master patterns. Tape stencil plastic over outline and trace all areas marked with No. 1; draw dotted lines around other areas as placement guides.

Remove and tape a second plastic sheet over outline. Trace all areas marked with No. 2; draw dotted lines as before.

Repeat for all other areas; there will be five stencils for the boy and six stencils for the girl. *Note:* Adjacent areas painted in same color are sometimes cut from different stencils to aid in shading.

Tape stencil materials to glass; cut only marked areas with knife.

COLOR KEY
1. Olive
2. Light Green
3. Blue Green
4. Light Burgundy
5. Dark Burgundy
6. Blue Print
7. Blue Dot

Spray foam-core board with adhesive; carefully place velveteen on board and smooth into place. *Note:* Nap of fabric goes downward.

MIXING COLORS: Mix colors on palette according to the following directions:

For skin, use white and flesh. For eyes, mix white and black to make gray. For cat, use white and black.

For girl's lips, use crimson and white; for boy's lips, use white and flesh.

For leaves, use green. For yarn ends, use Indian yellow.

For boy's suit and girl's belt, use blue and raw umber. For hair, use yellow ochre shaded with burnt umber. For dress and eyebrows, use dark brown. For flowers, yarn balls, and boy's tie, use crimson. For eyelashes, use black. For cheeks, use flesh painted with dry brush.

STENCILING THE PAINTINGS: *Note:* Practice painting, stenciling, and shading techniques on scrap of velveteen first. Center Stencil No. 1 over velveteen; tape in place. Lightly paint all areas of stencil using downward or upward motion in colors listed above. Gently rub paint into velveteen with stencil brush, shading darker areas.

Remove Stencil No. 1; repeat technique with Stencil No. 2, matching guidelines with painted areas. Continue with remaining areas. *Note:* Folds in skirt are made by placing edge of stencil plastic strip on each fold and gently painting.

FINISHING: Paint all finish lines by hand using brush dipped in turpentine and dabbed into appropriate color to make thin mixture. *Note:* Finish lines are shown in blue on patterns.

Allow painting to dry for several days before framing.

continued

——— Stencil Cutting Lines   Painted Detail Lines

VICTORIAN BOY PORTRAIT   **Full-Size Pattern**

— **Stencil Cutting Lines**   — **Painted Detail Lines**

VICTORIAN GIRL PORTRAIT   **Full-Size Pattern**

Victorian Baby Doll

Shown on page 13.

MATERIALS

Note: Fabrics are 45 inches wide
½ yard of muslin (body)
2½ yards of white embroidered eyelet (dress and bonnet)
1 yard of lightweight white fabric (dress bodice lining and slip)
Embroidery floss: 10 skeins of light rust (hair), and one skein *each* of dark gray, blue-gray, dark peach, peach, and white
Polyester fiberfill
4 yards of ¼-inch-wide white satin ribbon
½ yard of elastic cord
Powdered blush
Dressmaker's carbon *or* water-erasable marker
Doll needle; dental floss

INSTRUCTIONS

Note: All pieces include ¼-inch seam allowances unless otherwise noted. Sew all pieces right sides together and press and clip seam allowances unless otherwise noted.

Enlarge patterns on page 24 and cut out all pieces, except face, from appropriate fabric. *Note:* Cut dress bodice so bottom of bodice is along bordered edge of eyelet.

In addition, from eyelet, cut one 22x54-inch rectangle (skirt) and one 12¾x8½-inch rectangle (bonnet) with longest side along eyelet border. Cut two 9x11-inch rectangles (sleeves) from remaining eyelet. Cut one 26x38-inch rectangle (slip) from white fabric.

BODY AND LEGS: Sew center front and center back seams of body; set aside.

Sew heel and toe darts of each leg; trim. Sew legs together in pairs, leaving open at tops and between dots; turn to right side. At top of right leg, fold fabric flat and slide so that front seam falls ½ inch to right of back seam; baste in place. This completes the right leg. Repeat for left leg, reversing the process so front seam is to left of back seam.

Sew gathering stitches to tops of legs and pull to measure 2 inches. Sew legs to body front between dots. Sew body back to front, leaving open at neck. Turn to right side and stuff body firmly. Stuff legs firmly to within 1 inch of top. *Note:* Do not stuff top 1 inch of leg. Sew openings closed.

If desired, stitch heel dimples, using dental floss, by taking small stitch at one end of dart, pulling needle through foot to end of other dart. Pull floss tightly and knot. Stitch through knee 1 inch from front seam to create knee dimples. Soft-sculpt toes, if desired.

ARMS: Sew arms together in pairs, leaving open between dots. Turn to right side and stuff firmly to within 1 inch of top. *Note:* Do not stuff top 1 inch of arm. Slip-stitch openings closed. Tack one arm securely to each side of body 1⅛ inches from neck opening.

FACE AND HEAD: Trace face outline and features onto right side of muslin. Satin-stitch eyes with blue-gray floss and lips with dark peach. Straight-stitch eye accents with white and dark gray; straight-stitch eyelashes with peach. Stem-stitch eye outline with dark gray; stem-stitch eyebrows with peach. Color cheeks with blush. Cut out face.

Sew face dart and trim. Sew chin to face from dot to dot, matching centers. Sew center seam of head backs.

Sew head back to face and chin, keeping pointed seam allowances at dot free and leaving open at neck edge. Turn to right side; stuff firmly. Turn under ¾ inch on neck edges; sew body to head with dental floss.

HAIR: For each section, remove paper from one skein of floss and spread center of floss to measure 1¾ inches. Sew across center and cut each end. Tack one skein to head where dart and head seams meet. Repeat for remaining skeins, tacking to head back ½ inch from

previous skein. *Note:* Use several skeins for longer or thicker sections, such as above ears. Trim length as needed and gently comb and style the hair as desired.

SLIP: Sew fronts to backs at shoulders. To make lined bodice, sew bodice to lining along center back, neck, and armholes; turn to right side. Match side seams of lining and bodice, right sides together; sew.

Gather one long edge of skirt at waistline. Sew short edges together to within 5 inches of gathered edge for center back seam. Press edges of opening to wrong side; topstitch in place. Turn up 5¼-inch hem, turning under raw edge; hand- or machine-stitch hem.

Pull skirt gathers to fit bodice; sew together along stitching line. Press under seam allowance of bodice lining; hand-sew over stitching line, encasing raw edges. Tack ribbons at neck and bodice edges for closure.

DRESS: Sew fronts to backs at shoulders. To make lined bodice, sew bodice to lining at center back and neck; turn. Sew bodice side seams, then lining side seams, right sides together. Turn and press.

Baste bodice to lining at armhole edges, wrong sides together. Assemble skirt same as for slip, omitting hem. Gather edge to fit bodice; sew together. Tack or topstitch bodice lining over seam line, encasing raw edges.

Gather one wide edge of each sleeve. Turn under 1 inch on opposite edge. Place elastic on wrong side of hem, ¾ inch from folded edge. Zigzag-stitch over the elastic, keeping elastic free from stitches. Pull up elastic to fit wrist. Sew underarm seams, catching ends of the elastic in seam line to secure.

Gather the sleeves to fit the armhole edges, leaving underarm free of gathers. Sew the sleeves to the bodice. Tack ribbons at neck and bodice edges for closures.

continued

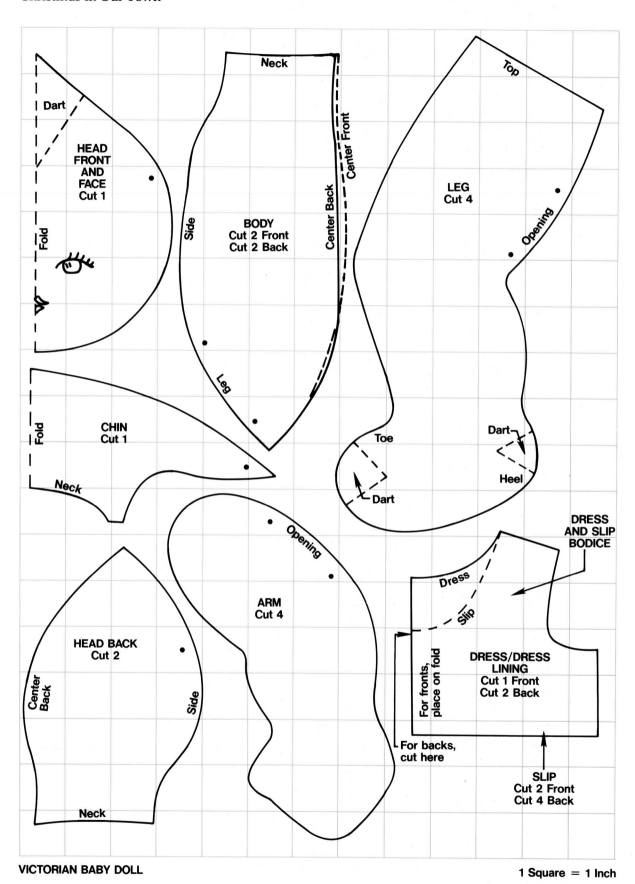

VICTORIAN BABY DOLL

1 Square = 1 Inch

BONNET: Cut a 12¾x2¾-inch strip (bonnet band) from bordered edge of eyelet, aligning scallop of eyelet with one long edge of rectangle. Narrowly hem short sides of band and bonnet. Stitch right side of band to wrong side of bonnet along cut edge. Turn band to right side of bonnet, encasing raw edges; press.

Press under ¾ inch of remaining raw edge; turn under raw edges. Sew along folded edge to form casing. Insert 20-inch length of satin ribbon through casing; pull up ribbon to fit doll's head and tie in bow. Trim ends of ribbon.

Tack long ribbons to front edges of bonnet; tie under doll's chin, allowing ribbons to drape.

Big and Little Sister Dolls

Shown on page 12.
Finished sizes are 15 and 18½ inches high.

MATERIALS

For small doll
¼ yard of cotton print (dress)
¼ yard of cotton (pantaloons)
¼ yard knit (stockings)

For large doll
½ yard of cotton print (dress)
½ yard of cotton (pantaloons)
½ yard knit (stockings)

For both dolls
1 yard of fabric (bodies)
String, cotton carpet warp, embroidery floss, *or* pearl cotton (hair)
Dark brown, medium blue, and medium rose embroidery floss
Scrap of soft leather (shoes)
Four ¾-inch buttons
Three small buttons
½ yard of scalloped edging
½ yard of ¼-inch-wide elastic
½ yard of narrow ribbon
¼ yard of embroidered trim
Scraps of fusible interfacing
Polyester fiberfill

INSTRUCTIONS

Note: Full-size patterns on pages 26–28 are for small doll; for larger doll, have pieces enlarged at a quick-print shop to 125 percent. Construction for both is identical.

Pattern pieces are finished size; add ¼-inch seam allowances to all pieces before cutting them from fabric. Cut out all pieces from appropriate fabrics. Unless otherwise noted, sew with right sides together.

LEGS AND ARMS: Fuse strips of interfacing to wrong sides of buttonhole markings on all leg and arm pieces to reinforce the buttonholes made later.

Sew the two leg pieces together, leaving open as marked. Repeat for other leg. Sew arms similarly. Clip all pieces and turn to the right side.

Topstitch along dotted line at top of arm and leg pieces. Make buttonholes to fit buttons where indicated.

Stuff arms and legs firmly; slip-stitch closed. Set aside.

HEAD: Fold face in half, wrong sides together, so dotted lines of nose match; backstitch along these lines with dark brown floss. Embroider eyebrows in running stitch with dark brown and eyes in blue French knots. Satin-stitch mouth with rose. Make small straight stitches for freckles with dark brown; see photograph on page 12.

Cut hair material to desired length for bangs and hair. Baste hair to head back between lines indicated on the pattern. Baste bangs between dots.

Pin head pieces right sides together, with hair to inside. Sew through all thicknesses, leaving open at neck edge. Reinforce along hairline. Turn to right side and stuff firmly.

BODY: Sew body front to back, leaving open at neck and bottom. To form inner leg, sew front to back along V-shaped dotted line at bottom opening; reinforce. Slash center of V from bottom to point.

Fold body so inner leg seam line and outer body seam line match. Sew across bottom opening. Repeat for other leg.

To square shoulders, fold upper body so shoulder seam line and outer body seam line meet and shoulder forms a triangle. Mark straight line across triangle, ¼ inch from point; stitch on line. Repeat for other shoulder.

Turn body to right side; stuff firmly. Turn body neckline seam allowances to inside. Slide neck into neck opening, matching side seams. Slip-stitch head to body.

Mark position for arm buttons by aligning top of arm with shoulder. Mark position for leg buttons by placing doll in sitting position so backs of legs are even with base of doll. Sew buttons at marks; button limbs to doll.

Pull hair slightly to back; tack to center back of head. Braid and tie with ribbon, or leave hair loose.

DRESS: *Note:* Instead of a collar, a 15-inch length of scalloped edging may be gathered into neckline.

Sew collar front to backs at shoulder seams; repeat for collar facings. Sew collar to facing, leaving neck edge open. Turn and press. Add crochet or lace trim, if desired.

Sew bodice front to back at shoulder seams; repeat for lining. Baste collar to bodice along neckline edge, matching shoulder seams. Sew bodice to lining along neckline and back edges, taking care not to catch collar in back seam. Turn to right side; press. Lift collar from bodice; edge-stitch neckline underneath collar. Baste bodice to lining at side and waistline seams, wrong sides together.

Sew sleeve to shoulder, matching dot to shoulder seam; repeat with second sleeve. Narrowly hem the sleeves. If desired, slip-stitch braid ¼ inch from hemmed edge. Fold sleeve in half lengthwise; sew underarm and side seams in one continuous line. Repeat for other side.

Lay bodice flat; lap left side over right by ½ inch and baste in place at waistline.

Cut an 8½x22-inch rectangle for small doll's skirt; cut a 10½x28-inch rectangle for large doll's skirt. Fold in half crosswise. Mark dot at top of

continued on page 28

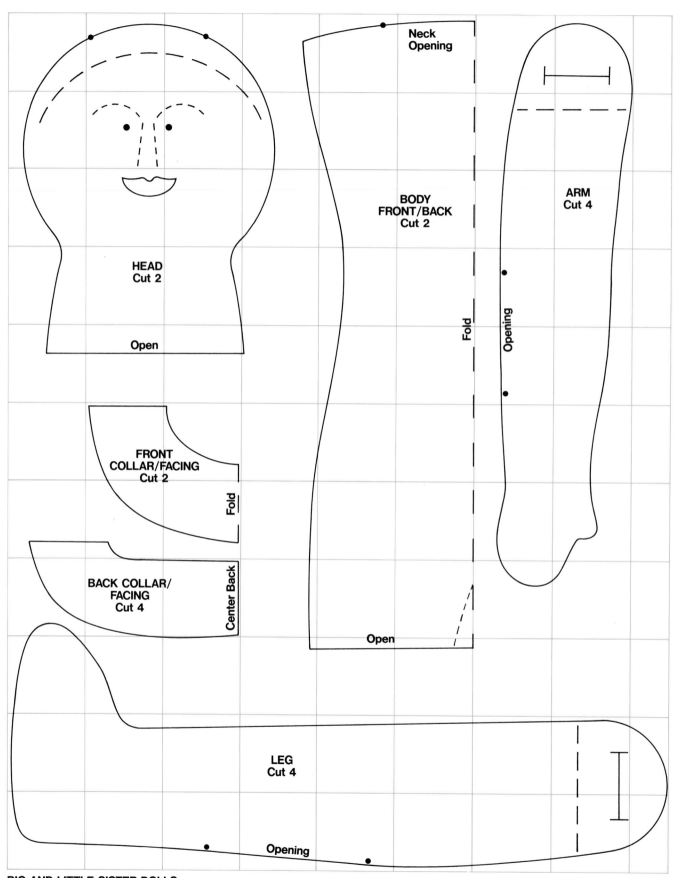

HEAD
Cut 2

Open

Neck
Opening

BODY
FRONT/BACK
Cut 2

Fold

Opening

Open

ARM
Cut 4

FRONT
COLLAR/FACING
Cut 2

Fold

BACK COLLAR/
FACING
Cut 4

Center Back

LEG
Cut 4

Opening

BIG AND LITTLE SISTER DOLLS

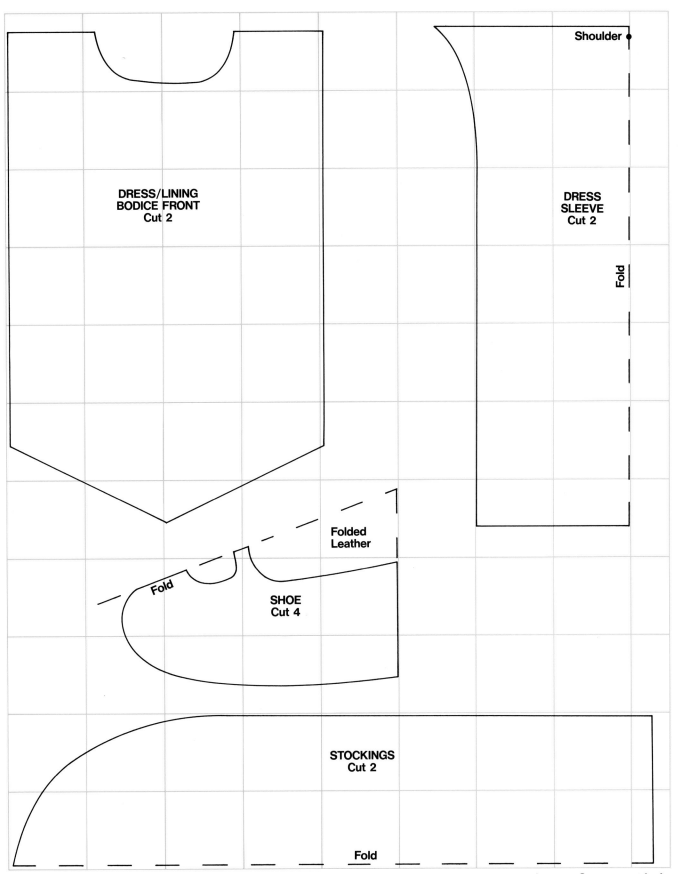

DRESS/LINING BODICE FRONT
Cut 2

Shoulder •

DRESS SLEEVE
Cut 2

Fold

Folded Leather

Fold

SHOE
Cut 4

STOCKINGS
Cut 2

Fold

Big Sister: 1 Square = 1 Inch
Little Sister: Full-Size Patterns

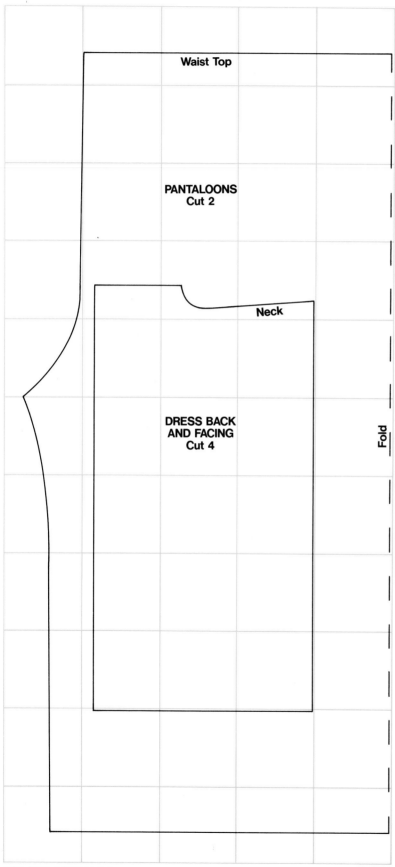

BIG AND LITTLE SISTER DOLLS

Big Sister: 1 Square = 1 Inch
Little Sister: Full-Size Patterns

fabric 6 inches (7½ inches for large doll) from folded edge; mark second dot along fold line, 1 inch (1¼ inches for large doll) from top edge. Connect dots with straight line. Cut on line, removing the triangular-shape piece of fabric.

Sew short ends together for center back seam. On straight edge, fold 3 inches (3¾ inches for large doll) to wrong side; sew ¼-inch (⅜-inch for large doll) tuck completely around skirt. Turn up 1 inch (1¼ inch for large doll); sew second line of tucking. Hem skirt to bottom row of tucks.

Along skirt waistline, stitch two rows of gathering threads; pull gathers to fit bodice. Sew skirt to bodice at waistline; press seam allowance toward bodice.

Sew small buttons and buttonholes or crocheted loops at back opening.

PANTALOONS: Narrowly hem legs. Trim with scalloped edging. Sew pieces together along center front seam. Turn under ⅜-inch (½-inch for large doll) waistline casing, turning raw edges to inside; sew in place. Cut elastic to fit doll's waist plus ½ inch; insert elastic through casing and secure.

Cut two pieces of elastic 5 inches (6½ inches for large doll) for ankles. Sew elastic ½ inch (⅝ inch for large doll) from hemmed edge of pantaloon, stretching elastic as you sew to create gathers. Repeat for other leg.

Sew center back seam of pantaloons. Sew inner leg seam in one continuous seam.

STOCKINGS AND SHOES: Sew curved edges in ¼-inch seam. *Note:* Stockings are designed to bag and roll slightly. Cut out shoes from leather. Sew sole and back seams. Cut out opening and strap as indicated on pattern.

Bear Pull Toy

Shown on page 12.

MATERIALS

14x24-inch piece of beige fur
Two 9-mm eyes
2x5-inch piece of hook-and-loop tape
Black embroidery floss
Polyester fiberfill
5x10-inch piece of ¾-inch oak
Four 2⅞-inch-diameter metal wheels (available at crafts supply stores)
¾ yard of ¼-inch-diameter cord
Eight small washers
Green acrylic paint
Varnish; wood filler; wood stain
3-inch length of ½-inch-diameter dowel; drill
Forty ¾-inch gold jingle bells
3 feet of florist's wire

INSTRUCTIONS

Note: All pieces, *except tail,* include ¼-inch seam allowances. Sew all pieces for bear with right sides facing unless otherwise noted.

BEAR: Enlarge patterns on page 30; transfer to back of fur. Transfer soles to hook-and-loop tape. Cut out all pieces except tail, making sure to reverse pieces and follow nap markings.

Sew body gusset pieces together along upper edge, leaving open between dots. Sew gusset to one body side, leaving open at bottom of legs; repeat for other side.

Sew chin and chest of bear, starting at dot and stopping at gusset.

Sew straight edge of nose gusset to nose; sew one side of head gusset to head. Repeat for other side. Insert eyes.

Sew back of bear from head gusset to body gusset; reinforce by stitching again. Sew loop portions of hook-and-loop tape soles to leg openings.

Turn bear; stuff firmly. Hand-sew opening closed. Sew ears together along curved edges; turn and sew openings closed. Sew ears on head, curving slightly. Clip fur on snout; embroider nose and mouth using six plies of floss.

Fold tail section on dotted line; sew on solid line, leaving open at bottom. Cut out and turn to right side. Hand-sew to bear as marked on pattern.

BASE: Paint wheels; set aside to dry. Sand and paint dowel.

Sand the oak base. Stain and varnish according to manufacturer's directions. Drill pilot holes for wheels 1½ inches from front and back ends. Drill ¼-inch hole through base at center front.

Nail wheels to base, inserting two washers between wheel and base. Insert cord through center front hole; tie on underside to secure.

Drill ¼-inch hole through center of dowel; insert free end of cord and knot to secure; trim ends.

Stand bear on base; mark position of feet. Glue hook portions of hook-and-loop tape to markings. When dry, place bear on base hook-and-loop tape.

COLLAR: Fold wire in half. Slide one bell down each end of wire. Twist wires together to secure bells. Slide another bell down each end of wire; twist. Repeat for remaining bells. Loop wire into circle; twist wire ends around end bell to secure. Slip over bear's head and adjust if necessary; trim ends.

Bell Stocking

Shown on page 15.

MATERIALS

⅜ yard of floral fabric *or* chintz
⅜ yard of muslin
½ yard of velvet
1½ yards of narrow cording
½ yard of ⅜-inch-wide decorative cording; jingle bells
⅜ yard of lightweight quilt batting
Gold metallic sewing thread

INSTRUCTIONS

Enlarge pattern on page 82.

Layer fabric, batting, and muslin; baste together. Plan position of front and back (one piece is reversed) on fabric. Machine-quilt around flower shapes with metallic thread.

Adding ½-inch seam allowances, cut out stocking front and back.

Make velvet piping and stitch to front along outline, omitting piping along top edge.

Place front and back right sides together; stitch around, leaving top open. Clip curves and turn.

Cut a 3- to 4-inch-deep cuff from velvet to fit around stocking top. Sew short ends of cuff together to form tube; finish lower edge of cuff.

Keeping cuff seam to back of stocking, pin right side of cuff to wrong side of top edge of stocking. Sew along top edge. Finish seams; turn cuff to right side.

Trim bottom of cuff with cording. Add jingle bells.

Patchwork Hearts

Shown on page 14.

MATERIALS

Old crazy quilt top cut into 7-inch square *or* new fabric assembled into similar patchwork
Scrap of muslin (backing)
½ yard of purchased cording
Polyester fiberfill; paper
Water-erasable marker

INSTRUCTIONS

Note: Use ½-inch seams and sew with right sides together.

For pattern, cut a 5x5-inch paper heart; trace onto quilt piece and muslin, adding seam allowances.

Baste cording to stitching line of heart. Sew backing to front, leaving opening for turning. Clip curves and turn. Stuff with fiberfill and close.

Mitten Ornament

Shown on page 14.

MATERIALS

One square of felt
Scrap of fusible interfacing
5 inches of ¾-inch-wide pregathered lace
Green embroidery floss; scraps of floss in light and dark colors
3-inch hair clip; glue

continued

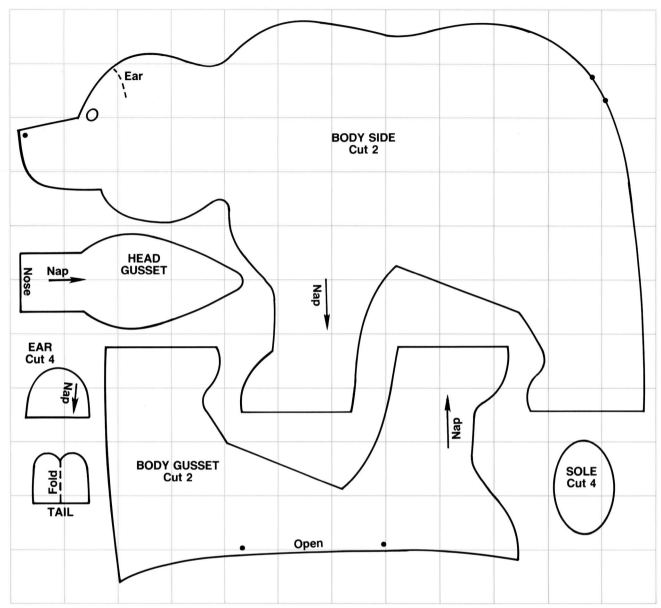

BEAR PULL-TOY

1 Square = 1 Inch

INSTRUCTIONS

Note: Each ornament consists of four felt mitten shapes (stitched together in pairs to form two mittens) connected by a hair clip inserted into each finished mitten.

Cut the felt square into four 4x5-inch pieces.

Fuse interfacing to the backs of two of the rectangles for tops of each pair.

Trace mitten outline on page 31 onto interfaced rectangles. Embroider the mitten tops. The leaves are stitched in lazy daisy stitches using green floss. For the flowers, choose two shades of floss for the flowers, such as light pink and dark pink or light blue and dark blue. The flower centers are stitched in French knots using the light floss. The petals are stitched in bullion stitches using the dark floss.

Cut the lace in half; pin to wrong side of mitten tops at wrist with lace extending to form cuff. Topstitch the lace in place.

Pin remaining rectangles to wrong side of interfaced rectangles. Sew along outline, leaving open at lace edge. Trim seam closely; trim lace.

Glue one inner edge of the hair clip to one inner mitten; allow to dry. Repeat for the remaining mitten. Clip to tree branch to hang.

Embroidered Glove Ornaments

Shown on page 14.

MATERIALS

For each glove

8x8-inch piece of ecru polished cotton or muslin

4x8-inch scrap of batting

6 inches of 1¾-inch-wide lace, pregathered along one side

4 inches of 1½-inch-wide lace, pregathered down center

18 inches of ⅜-inch-wide picot-edge ribbon in dark color

10 inches of ⅛-inch-wide satin ribbon in light color

Dark ecru thread

Small bouquet of artificial flowers and leaves to match ribbons

INSTRUCTIONS

Fold fabric in half, right sides together. Transfer full-size pattern, *below,* to fabric. Pin batting to wrong side of fabric.

Stitch outline of glove through all three layers, leaving an opening at wrist edge. Trim seams and clip curves; turn to right side and press.

Topstitch finger lines with dark ecru thread. Using double strand of dark thread, featherstitch lines as indicated on pattern.

MITTEN ORNAMENTS　　　　　　　　**Full-Size Pattern**

Trim batting. Turn under wrist edge and slip-stitch closed.

Hem the cut edges of edge-gathered lace. Sew additional gathering threads along gathering line. Pin lace to front of glove at wrist with lace extending upward to form cuff and ¼ inch turned to back. Pull gathers to fit glove; stitch in place.

Pin remaining lace around wrist and ¼ inch below first lace strip. Blindstitch in place along gathering.

Cut picot-edge ribbon to fit wrist; sew over center of second lace strip. Make double bow (four loops) with

satin ribbon; tack to center front of wrist. Make slightly smaller double bow with remaining picot-edge ribbon; tack on top of first bow.

Tack flowers over centers of bows. Trim ends of ribbon.

Fan hemmed edges of lace cuff to meet wrist in back; tack in place. Make loop for hanging from remaining satin ribbon; tack in place at center back.

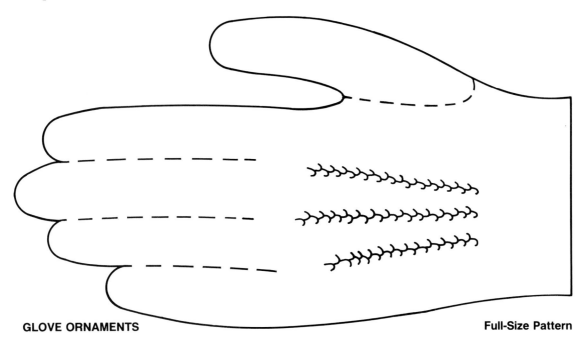

GLOVE ORNAMENTS　　　　　　　　**Full-Size Pattern**

Season's Greetings in Cross-Stitch

Twinkling candles, festive greenery, and a starry sky are some of the beautiful images we look forward to seeing every Christmas, and you'll find each one on this holiday banner.

The cross-stitch banner, *right,* is a timeless decoration that you'll want to display every year. Although you'll need only five colors of floss to make it, imaginative use of surface pattern, striking shapes, and graceful lettering all combine to create an effective design.

To make this 19x15-inch banner, refer to the chart on pages 34–35. You'll need a 21x25-inch piece of 11-count white Aida cloth and floss in colors listed in the color key. You'll need three skeins of the blue floss, one skein of the red, green, and yellow, and a small amount of the gray.

Prepare the fabric for stitching by binding its edges with masking tape. Measure three inches down from the top and three inches in from the left-hand edge and, using green floss, begin stitching here. To make the cross-stitches, use

two plies of embroidery floss and work each stitch over one thread of the fabric.

Work all of the border with green first and then add the blue sky, candles, lettering, and other design elements.

After the stitching is completed, steam-press it on the wrong side.

To assemble the stitchery into a banner, trim the fabric one inch beyond the stitching. Stitch red piping to the side and bottom edges, leaving two threads of fabric exposed between the stitches and the piping. With right sides facing, stitch the panel to a piece of lining fabric and stitch along the piping line again, leaving an opening for turning. Turn the banner to the right side, press, and slip-stitch the opening closed. Slip-stitch a casing to the back top edge and slide a 19-inch length of dowel into the casing for hanging.

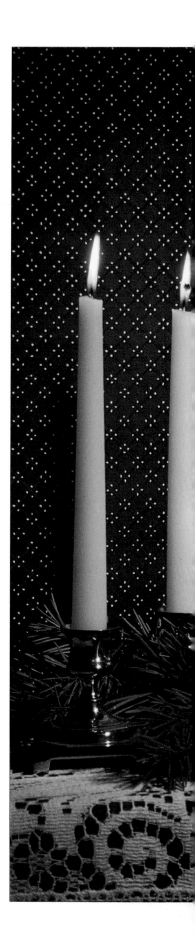

1 Square = 1 Cross-Stitch

COLOR KEY

■ No. 824 Blue   ■ No. 904 Parrot green   ■ No. 321 Christmas red

34

☐ No. 725 Topaz ■ No. 844 Beaver gray

Folk-Style Santas

Although he's changed over the years, Santa Claus remains an American folk creation. Here are six versions of that jolly, old elf to make yourself.

The delightful fellow, *left*, is clothed in red wool trimmed with white fur. Cover a plastic foam ball with packaged papier-mâché for his head, then pad and wrap a wire armature to make his body. Santa's sleigh is made from a pine scrap and lengths of half-round molding, and you can fill it with miniatures, holiday greens, or presents.

Use a new or slightly weathered board to make the cutout Santa, *above*. Transfer the outline and details to the piece of lumber, cut out and paint the figure, and mount it on a base.

Instructions for the six Santas in this chapter begin on page 40.

In Victorian times, Santa often wore a white robe. The cotton Santa, *opposite,* has a paper cutout face, a feature common to Victorian ornaments. Assemble him from batting pieces that have been "aged" with coffee.

Nearing a chimney with a tree and a bag of goodies, the wooden Santa, *opposite,* duplicates the look of sculpture with flat pieces of wood. Add texture with sponge-painted white fur and snow.

The cherry-cheeked wooden figure, *above,* shows Santa in profile. His arm, a piece secured to the body on a short dowel, can be rotated to any position.

Dummy boards like the one, *right,* were used as whimsical substitutes for people in large Victorian homes. Cut this St. Nick from distressed pine and add painted details.

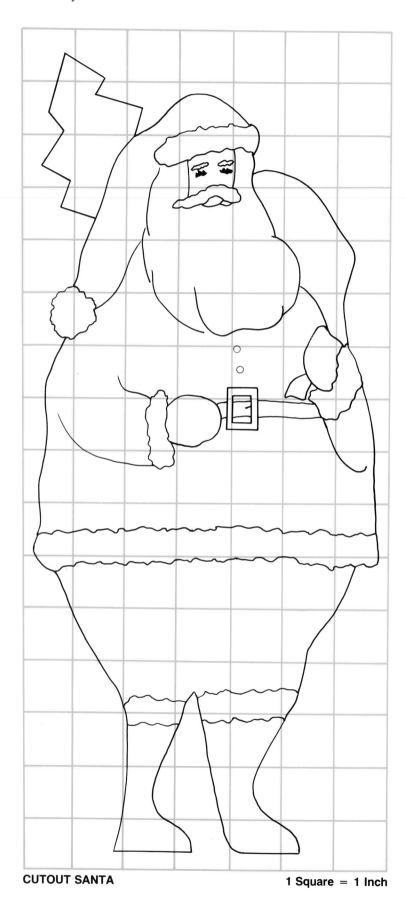

CUTOUT SANTA   **1 Square = 1 Inch**

Cutout Santa
Shown on page 37.
Finished size is 16x6¾x1½ inches.

MATERIALS
1½x6¾-inch piece of 1-inch pine
  (base)
8x16-inch piece of 1-inch pine
  (Santa)
Band saw with ⅛-inch blade
Sandpaper
Acrylic paints
Graphite paper
Paintbrushes
Wood glue
Wood screws
Burnt umber oil paint
Turpentine; rags
Matte-finish spray varnish

INSTRUCTIONS
Enlarge the pattern, *left,* onto heavy paper; cut out. Draw around paper pattern onto the larger piece of pine and cut out the Santa shape with a band saw or jigsaw. Sand all edges and surfaces smooth.

Leaving face plain, paint remaining surface of Santa shape red. Transfer beard, hair, body, clothing, and tree pattern details onto Santa. (*Note:* Transfer the details to the shape freehand or use graphite paper and press *lightly* onto the painted shape.)

Referring to the photograph on page 37 as a guide for color placement, paint the details of the Santa shape. Use darker colors first and finish with white. Paint the facial features over bare wood.

Paint the base green. Glue and screw the Santa's feet to the base. Seal the cutout and base with two coats of spray varnish.

To give the Santa an antique finish, dilute the oil paint with turpentine to create a very thin wash. Using rags and a light touch, quickly wipe the wash across the painted surface. Let the wash set for a few minutes and wipe away the excess with a clean rag. Wipe away more wash around the Santa's face and hands to emphasize these areas. Seal Santa again with additional coats of spray varnish.

Sleigh Santa

Shown on page 36.
Finished size is 16¾x10x13½ inches.

MATERIALS

For the head
1-inch-diameter plastic foam ball
2-inch-diameter plastic foam ball
Golf tee
1x3-inch piece of lightweight
  cardboard (rolled into a tube
  crosswise and taped)
Crafts glue; gesso
One package of papier-mâché
Fine sandpaper; antique glaze
Fine-tipped black marker
Flesh, red, white, and blue acrylic
  paints
Artist's brush

For the body
One 30-inch length of 18-gauge
  wire (body)
One 18-inch length of 18-gauge
  wire (arm span)
Polyester fiberfill
½ yard of 18-inch-wide fleece
Crafts glue; sewing thread
⅓ yard of white T-shirt knit fabric

For the clothing
Purchased 2½-inch black plastic
  boots (from crafts supply store)
Tan felt square (mittens)
¼ yard of navy suede cloth
  (pants)
⅛ yard of white fake fur
⅜ yard of red wool (coat and hat)
1 yard of ⅛-inch-diameter red
  cord
15-inch length of ½-inch-wide
  black belting; ½-inch buckle
White wool roving
½-inch jingle bell; fabric glue

For the sack
9x20-inch piece of brown fake fur
⅔ yard of ¼-inch-diameter red
  cord

For the sleigh
6x9-inch piece of 1-inch pine
14 feet of ⅝-inch half-round wood
  molding
1-inch brads; sandpaper; twine
Wood glue; saw; gray wood stain
continued

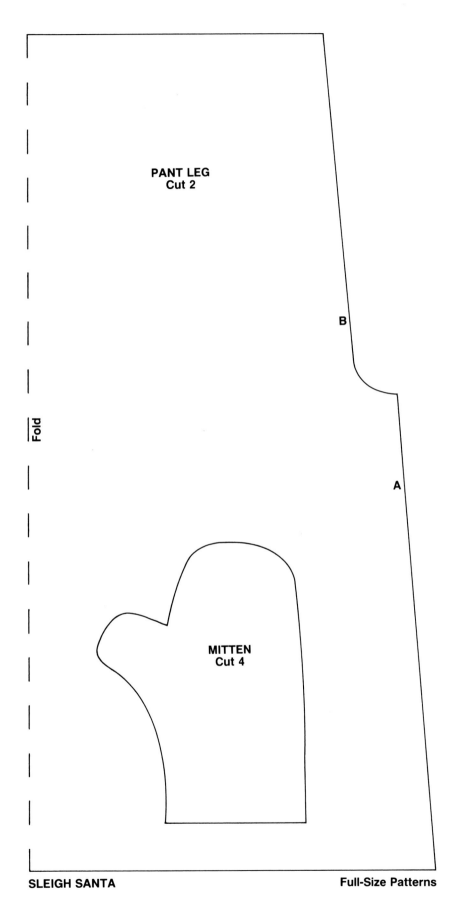

SLEIGH SANTA   **Full-Size Patterns**

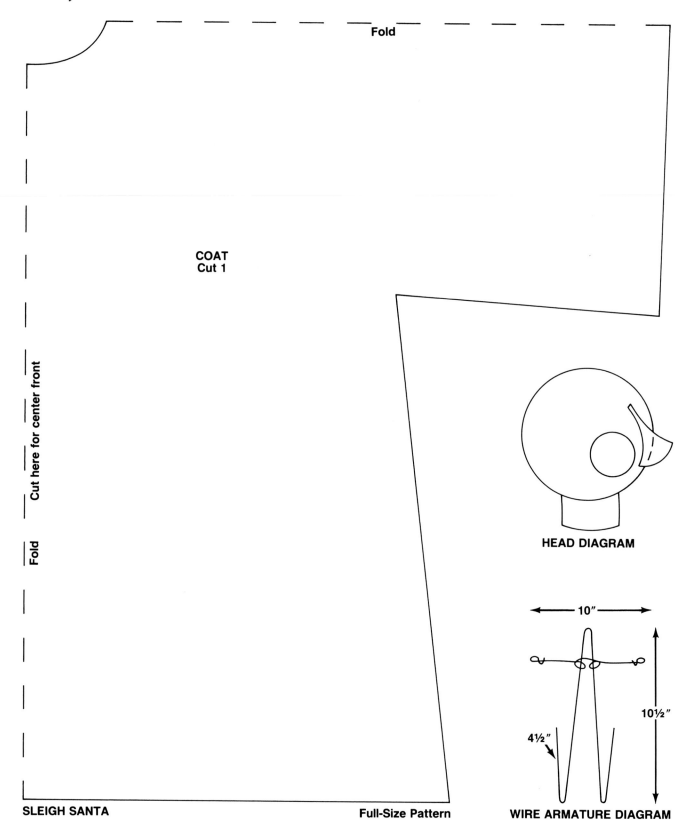

Fold

COAT
Cut 1

Cut here for center front

Fold

HEAD DIAGRAM

SLEIGH SANTA

Full-Size Pattern

10″

10½″

4½″

WIRE ARMATURE DIAGRAM

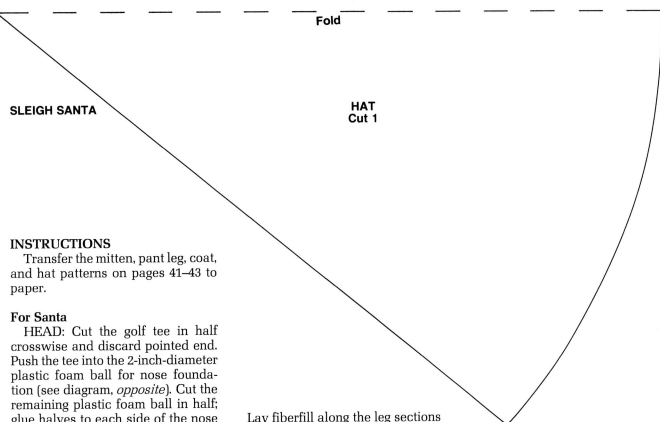

Fold

SLEIGH SANTA

HAT
Cut 1

Full-Size Pattern

INSTRUCTIONS

Transfer the mitten, pant leg, coat, and hat patterns on pages 41–43 to paper.

For Santa

HEAD: Cut the golf tee in half crosswise and discard pointed end. Push the tee into the 2-inch-diameter plastic foam ball for nose foundation (see diagram, *opposite*). Cut the remaining plastic foam ball in half; glue halves to each side of the nose for cheeks. Push cardboard tube ⅜ inch into head for the neck.

Prepare papier-mâché according to package directions. Coat head with papier-mâché; let dry. Sand lightly; apply another thin coat.

When the head is completely dry, sand it lightly and paint it with gesso. Paint the head and neck with flesh-colored acrylic paints. Paint the eyes blue and outline them with the black marker. Add a white dot to each eye to create a highlight. Use a thin wash of red paint to color the cheeks.

When the paint is dry, apply a coat of antique glaze with a rag.

BODY: Make a wire armature following inset diagram, *opposite*. Push top of body armature 1½ inches into bottom of head through neck tube; stuff neck with fiberfill.

To give body shape, pad 5 inches of armature below neck with fiberfill to form torso. Wrap fiberfill with thread to secure it in place. Use extra fiberfill to shape stomach and posterior. Continue to add and wrap fiberfill until the stomach measures 11½ inches in circumference.

Lay fiberfill along the leg sections of wire, tapering near bottoms; secure with thread. Slip a leg end into a boot to check fit; add more fiberfill to leg if necessary.

Cut the fleece into ½-inch-wide strips and wrap the torso and legs to make a smooth shape; glue ends of fleece to secure them.

Pad the arms with fiberfill in the same manner; secure with thread. Wrap arms with ½-inch-wide fleece strips.

Cut two 3x5½-inch white knit rectangles. Wrap a rectangle tightly around each arm; overlap and fold under one long edge; whipstitch. Gather bottom edge around wire; secure with thread. Tack top edge of knit to torso.

Wrap the legs as for arms using two 4x6-inch knit rectangles.

Wrap the torso tightly with a 7x10-inch knit rectangle, overlapping edges on one side of the body around one arm; pin. Slit knit down 1½ inches on opposite side to fit around arm. Tack edges of knit fabric together between the legs. Whipstitch the side edges together up to underarm. Turn under raw edges around arms; fit and stitch to body.

Overlap top edges to fit neck; whipstitch shoulders. Secure knit at neck with glue. Turn under raw edges and whipstitch around legs.

For Santa's clothing

Using the patterns, cut clothing from appropriate fabrics as listed in the materials list on page 41. Patterns include seam allowances. Sew pieces using a scant ¼-inch seam and with rights sides facing.

MITTENS: Sew mitten fronts to backs; trim and clip seam; turn right side out. Stuff mittens with fiberfill. Slip mittens onto arms; glue in place.

PANTS: Sew front and back seams first (along edge B), then sew inner leg seam (along edge A). Turn to right side; place on the Santa; turn under top raw edge; stitch to body. Gather pant legs 1¼ inches from bottom. Fill each boot bottom with fiberfill; place boots over leg ends and glue.

continued

Cut 2

Drill hole

CHERRY-CHEEKED SANTA

1 Square = 1 Inch

COAT: Sew coat side/sleeve seams; finish bottom edge with a 1-inch hem. Turn sleeves under ¼ inch; glue. Glue ¾-inch-wide fake-fur strips to left side of front, neckline, and hemline. Trim sleeves with ½-inch-wide fake-fur strips. Glue the ⅛-inch-wide red cord around sleeves and hemline, just above fur. Put coat on Santa, overlapping in front; glue.

BELT: Attach buckle to end of belt; angle-cut other end. Glue in place.

BEARD: Glue wool roving to face for beard and eyebrows. For mustache, tie center of twisted length of roving with thread; glue it in place.

HAT: Sew center seam. Turn under raw edge; stitch. Trim with a ¾-inch-wide fake-fur strip; add a bell to tip. Glue on head.

SACK: Fold fabric in half crosswise; stitch side seams ½ inch from raw edges. Turn right side out. Fold top edge 3 inches toward inside; tack in place. Stuff sack bottom with fiberfill; fill as desired.

For the sleigh

From molding cut the following: Four 5½-inch lengths (side supports), four 3¾-inch lengths (runner braces), two 16½-inch lengths (runners), six 9¾-inch lengths (side rails), and three 7-inch lengths (back rails). Sand the base and cut ends.

Glue and nail side supports perpendicular to long edges of base. Leave 7 inches between supports on each side and let 1½ inches of base extend on back end of sleigh. Angle-cut front end of each runner with a saw; sand. Glue and nail runner braces perpendicular to runners. Leave 5 inches between braces, placing first brace 6½ inches from front of each runner. Attach braced runners to sleigh base.

Stain all sleigh pieces; let dry.

Nail three side rails to each set of side supports, with a ⅝-inch space between rails. Glue back rails at sleigh rear; lash twine over joints.

continued

SAINT NICK DUMMY BOARD

Full-Size Pattern

Match line AB

B

A

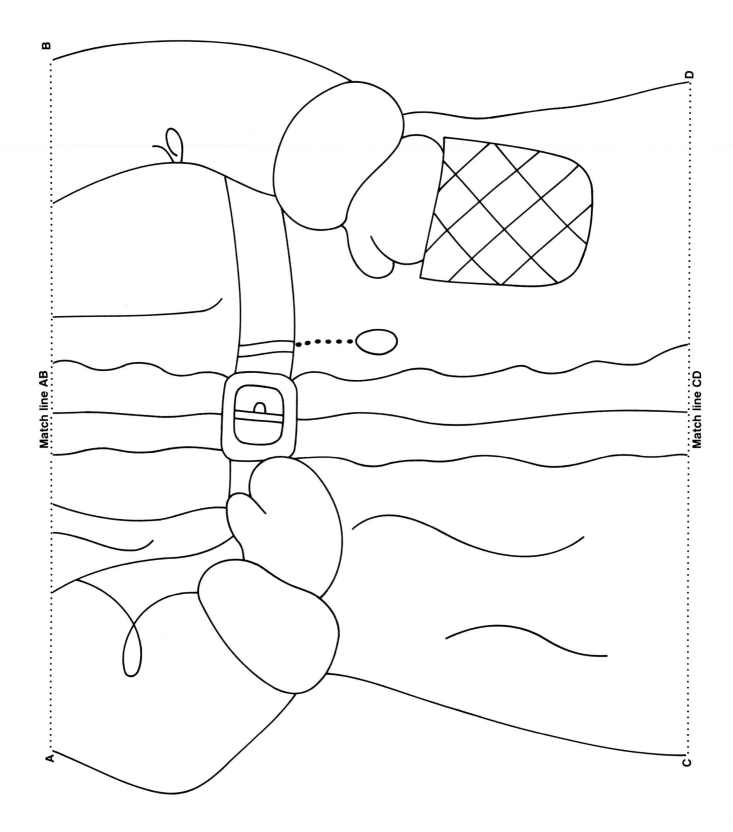

Match line AB

Match line CD

B

D

A

C

SAINT NICK DUMMY BOARD

Full-Size Pattern

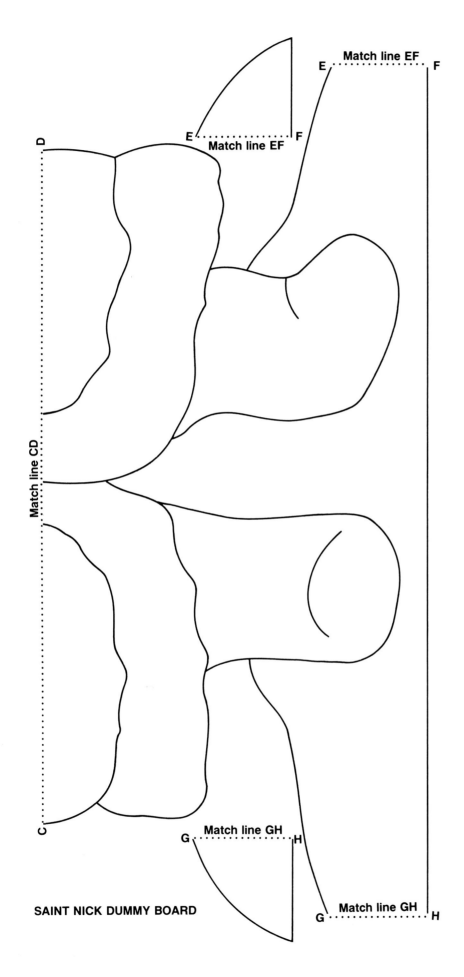

Match line EF

E............F

Match line EF

D

Match line CD

Match line GH

G............H

C

Match line GH

G............H

SAINT NICK DUMMY BOARD

Cherry-Cheeked Santa

Shown on page 39.
Finished size is 11x15x5 inches.

MATERIALS
5x11-inch piece of 1-inch pine
(base)
11x15-inch piece of 1-inch pine
(Santa)
Band saw with ⅛-inch blade
Sandpaper; wood file; drill
Red, white, brown, black, medium
blue, dark green, gold, and
peach acrylic paints
Paintbrushes; wood glue
Burnt umber oil paint
One 2-inch length and one 3-inch
length of ¼-inch-diameter
dowel; matte-finish varnish
Graphite paper; turpentine; rags

INSTRUCTIONS
Enlarge pattern on page 44.
Cut out and paint as for Saint
Nick Dummy Board; see page 48.
Use the shorter dowel to attach
arm piece to body. Glue in place.
Secure to base with longer dowel
as for Saint Nick Dummy Board; see
page 48. Seal Santa with varnish.

Saint Nick Dummy Board

Shown on page 39.
Finished size is 14x17x4½ inches.

MATERIALS
4x14-inch piece of 1-inch pine
(base)
11x17½-inch piece of 1-inch pine
(Santa)
Band saw with ⅛-inch blade
Red, white, brown, black, medium
blue, dark green, gold, and light
peach acrylic paints
Paintbrushes
Burnt umber oil paint
2½-inch length of ¼-inch-diameter
wood dowel; wood glue
Graphite paper; turpentine; rags
Drill with ¼-inch bit
Matte-finish varnish; sandpaper

continued

INSTRUCTIONS

Transfer the Saint Nick Dummy Board pattern on pages 45–47 onto paper. To complete the base shape, align the rounded points at lines EF and GH.

Trace shape onto pine board and cut out. Sand all edges and surfaces until smooth.

Paint the Santa red except for face; let dry. Transfer pattern detail onto Santa with graphite paper; use a light touch and take care not to indent the wood surface. Paint, using photograph on page 39 as a guide and using dark colors first. Add white details last.

Paint the base green; let dry.

Dilute burnt umber paint with turpentine to make a wash. Brush a thin coat of wash over both pieces. Remove excess wash with a turpentine-saturated rag; wipe again with a clean rag. Repeat procedure until desired antique shading is achieved. Let dry for at least 24 hours.

Cut the length of dowel in half. Drill two ¼-inch-diameter holes 3 inches apart in Santa's center bottom edge. Drill corresponding holes in base center. Glue dowels in Santa; set remaining dowel ends into the base. Varnish.

Cotton Santa

Shown on page 38.

MATERIALS

Cotton batting (80 percent cotton/20 percent polyester)
Santa face (cut from wrapping paper or greeting card)
Tongue depressor
Whole cloves
Red string
Glue gun or white glue
Instant coffee; spray bottle

INSTRUCTIONS

Cut an 11x15-inch rectangle from batting for the body. Cut one 8x11-inch rectangle for arms, and one 4½x6½-inch rectangle for the hat. Cut two 3x4-inch rectangles for the cuffs.

To antique the batting pieces, mix 1 teaspoon of instant coffee with 2 cups of hot water; cool. Pour solution into a spray bottle. Spray one side of each batting piece; dry. Turn; spray the other side, avoiding saturation. Let dry.

BODY: On body piece mark bottom and sides as follows: From the bottom right corner measure up 1 inch; mark this point with a dot. From the bottom right corner measure over 4 inches; mark this point with a dot. Draw a slightly curved line between these two dots; cut along the curved line. Repeat for the other side.

ARMS: Roll the arm rectangle lengthwise into cylinder; whipstitch the long raw edge to underlying layer to secure. Fold cuffs in half by turning long edges to middle; wrap cuffs around end of each arm. Whipstitch ends of each cuff together and tack to arms.

HAT: Fold hat piece in half to make a 4½x3¼-inch rectangle; stitch across one short end. Turn right side out and flatten with open seam at center back. Fold front edge back ½ inch twice. Hand-sew center back seam. Pad with excess batting in back under and behind brim.

FINISHING: Glue face on tongue depressor; glue hat onto head. Fold top of coat down 1 inch twice for collar. Position tongue depressor body inside coat with hat touching collar. Fold left side over depressor and glue. Turn raw edge of right side under and fold to overlap left front side. Glue at top and bottom. Center arm piece to coat back just below collar; glue. Bring arms around to front; stitch edges of cuffs together. Glue cloves to coat for buttons.

Chimney Santa

Shown on page 38.
Finished size is 13¾x14x2¾ inches.

MATERIALS

One 12x18-inch piece of 1-inch pine (rooftop and Santa)
18-inch piece of pine 2x4 (base and chimney)
One 8x12-inch piece of ¼-inch plywood (arms)
Band saw with ⅛-inch blade
Acrylic paints; paintbrushes
Carbon paper
Walnut oil-base wood stain
Small piece of sponge
Wood glue; sandpaper
Satin-finish spray varnish

INSTRUCTIONS

Enlarge patterns, *opposite,* and transfer onto heavy paper; cut out. Draw around patterns onto wood pieces; cut out. For the rooftop, cut a 2¾x12-inch rectangle from 1-inch pine. Sand all edges and surfaces of the pieces.

Paint one side of the rooftop brown. Glue rooftop, brown side up, to sloping edge of base. Referring to the photograph on page 38 paint both sides of Santa pieces as desired, *except* for fur trim and beard.

To paint fur, dilute white paint until it is the consistency of heavy cream. Dip the sponge into the paint, and then tap away the excess paint on paper towels. Using an up-and-down dabbing motion, *lightly* paint fur areas white. Sponge-paint snow onto green tree similarly.

Paint chimney dark red; outline bricks with gray. When dry, sand *lightly* to achieve a worn look.

To assemble, glue arms to body, referring to photograph on page 38 for placement. Glue chimney to rooftop, placing short end 1 inch in from high rooftop edge. *Note:* Santa will be stepping onto higher end of chimney. Glue Santa to rooftop so elevated foot rests on chimney edge. Seal with varnish.

CHIMNEY SANTA

Base

1 Square = 2 Inches

Festive Patchwork in Christmas Colors

A cheery quilt in the Kansas Troubles pattern—called Irish Puzzle by some—is a perfect choice for a Christmas coverlet.

Though Pine Tree and Star designs are the traditional choices for holiday patchwork projects, the strong graphic quality and classic color scheme of this lively old pattern make it a perfect foil for holiday decorating. Add a pair of forest green shams and a few lace pillows and—voilà—your guest room is all dressed up for Christmas.

Despite its woeful name, the Kansas Troubles pattern, using simple squares and triangles, is no trouble at all to piece. Once completed, the design can be outline-quilted either by hand or by machine, as time and fancy dictate.

The quilt pictured here is a treasured 19th-century antique, but it's quite at home in any setting, from early American to stark contemporary. Since the pattern itself is so strong, a no-frills backdrop is best, one in which the quilt is showcased as the pièce de résistance.

51

Kansas Troubles Quilt

Shown on pages 50–51.
Finished block is 16x16 inches.
Finished quilt is 70x88 inches.

MATERIALS

4 yards of red fabric
3½ yards of white fabric
6 yards of backing fabric
¾ yard of fabric (binding)
Quilt batting
Cardboard or plastic for templates

INSTRUCTIONS

Preshrink, dry, and press all fabrics before cutting the pieces.

Trace and make templates for the pattern pieces, *below.* Label each template and mark each with arrows indicating fabric grain direction. The pattern pieces shown are finished size; add ¼-inch seam allowances when cutting pieces from fabric.

To cut out the patchwork pieces, draw *lightly* around templates onto the *wrong* side of the fabric with a hard-lead pencil; cut out the pieces.

Store the pieces (sorted by color and shape) in a plastic bag or envelope until you are ready to use them.

CUTTING INSTRUCTIONS: From the white fabric, cut 80 A triangles, 480 B triangles, and 92 C squares (80 for the quilt blocks and 12 for the sashing squares).

From the red fabric, cut 80 A triangles and 480 B triangles. Cut 31 sashing strips, each 2½x16½ inches; the measurements for the sashing strips include ¼-inch seam allowances.

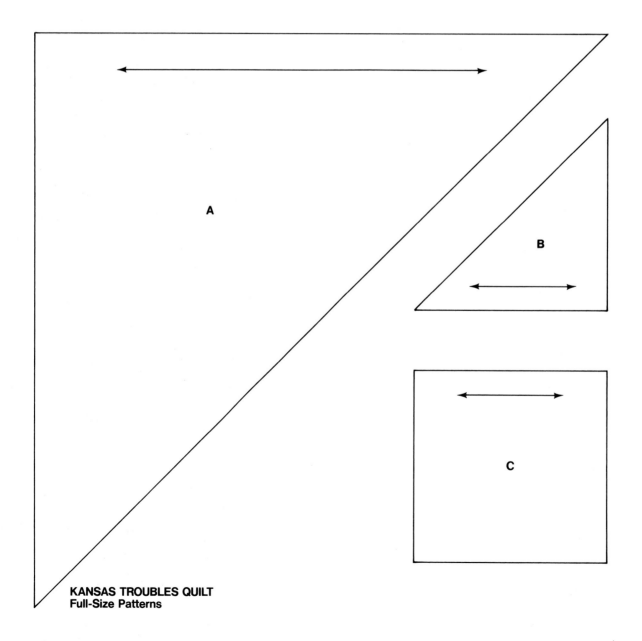

KANSAS TROUBLES QUILT
Full-Size Patterns

TO PIECE THE BLOCK: Begin by making the quarter blocks. To make one quarter block, refer to Figure 1, *below left.* Sew a red A triangle and a white A triangle together, stitching along the long sides, to make a square. Make six pairs of B triangle-squares similarly.

Referring to diagram for color position, join three B triangle-squares together to form a strip, adding a C square to one end of one of the strips.

Sew the shorter strip to one of the sides of the A triangle-square, and sew the remaining strip to the adjacent side of the A triangle-square and to the end of the first strip. The finished size of a quarter block is 8½x8½ inches, which includes the seam allowances.

To make one quilt block, piece four quarter blocks. Referring to Figure 2, *below right,* stitch four quarter blocks into a block.

Make 20 blocks.

TO MAKE THE QUILT TOP: Join four blocks and three sashing strips in a horizontal row, placing a sashing strip between the blocks. Make five rows of blocks.

To make a sashing row, join four sashing strips and three white C squares in a horizontal row, placing a square between the strips. Make four rows of sashing strips.

Beginning and ending with a row of blocks, alternately join rows of blocks and rows of sashing strips.

FINISHING: To piece the quilt back, cut or tear the backing fabric into two long panels. Split one panel in

half lengthwise. Using ½-inch seam allowances and matching selvage edges, sew a half panel to each side of the full panel. Trim selvages so seam allowances are approximately ¼ inch. Press seams to one side.

Layer the quilt top, batting, and backing; baste the layers together. Outline-quilt ¼ inch from all seams, and add other quilting, if desired. From the binding fabric, cut approximately 10 yards of 2½-inch-wide binding; cut the binding on either the bias or the straight grain. Press the binding in half so it is 1¼ inches wide. Matching raw edges, sew the binding to the quilt. Trim the excess batting and backing. Turn the folded edge of the binding to the quilt back and stitch.

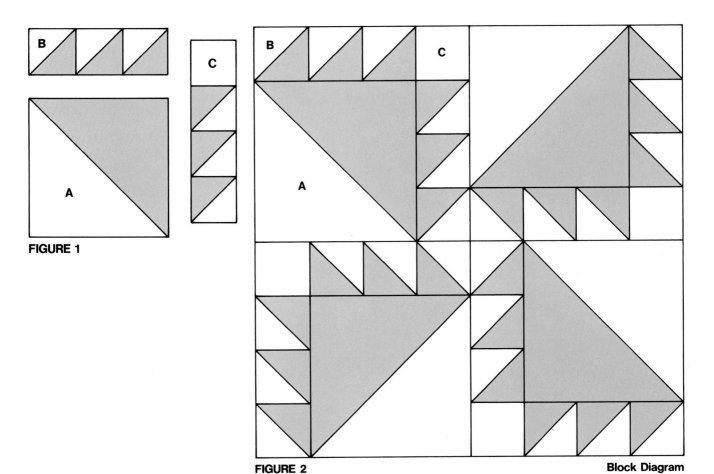

FIGURE 1

FIGURE 2

Block Diagram

A Southwest-Style Holiday

A palette of vibrant colors, imaginative use of natural materials, and designs based on bold, simple shapes are the trademarks of Southwest style found in this collection of lively decorations and gifts.

Turquoise and silver inspired the tree, *left*, trimmed with balls, popcorn, and painted bead necklaces.

Use inexpensive fringed serapes for the stockings, *left,* or substitute striped wool.

Strip piecing that results in diagonal rows of colorful squares is used for the quilt.

The doll and angel ornament, *above,* are two versions of the same pattern. Both are made from felt.

Instructions begin on page 64.

The stately crèche figures, *below,* are elegant soft-sculpture pieces to display beneath the tree or on a tabletop. Choose remnants of rich-looking fabrics to make them, and aim for an interesting mix of striped, paisley, and linen scraps. To make the halos, string small beads onto wires shaped into circles and attach them to the figures' heads.

The wood and tin wreath, *opposite,* is an easy and everlasting design that resembles the popular work of Mexican tinsmiths. Cut out leaf shapes from sheet aluminum and nail them to the black plywood wreath shape. Add borders of upholstery tacks, and antique the shiny metal with a wash of black paint.

The candle holders perched on the window, *opposite,* are formed from lengths of wire. Wrap one end of the wire around a broomstick to make a cylindrical holder, and then bend the other end of the wire downward at a right angle. String wooden beads onto the wire for balance, and stabilize the holders on a windowsill or a shelf with pushpins.

A host of heavenly angels decorates the tree, *opposite* and *right.* These angel ornaments (see the larger, doll version on page 55) are stitched from felt cut into basic shapes. Special details on these ornaments include narrow black satin ribbon used for hair, a reindeer and tree motif stitched onto the skirt in half cross-stitches, and a pair of lacy paper wings.

For the toy drum ornaments, *opposite,* begin with a large-size tuna can. Remove the bottom, and cover the outside with adhesive vinyl. Stencil-paint circles of chamois for the drums' tops and bottoms, and lace them in place with string.

Riotous combinations of fabrics, laces, ribbons, and other trims are the materials you'll need for the rag ball ornaments, *opposite* and *right.* Organize the scraps by basic color, and then just pin them to a plastic foam ball.

As a finishing touch for this tree of ornaments, drape lengths of ¼- to ½-inch-wide grosgrain ribbons in deep swags on the branches.

In arid locales, ears of Indian corn can make a handsome substitute for more traditional greenery. For the wreath, *left,* leave the husks on the ears and wire them to a wreath form. Add dried chilies for accents, and fill in empty spaces with extra husks.

A single bird, *above,* or the fabric flock on the tree on page 54 look serenely at home amid the evergreens. Look in your scrap bag for the makings.

Begin with inexpensive clear glass tumblers to make the candle holders, *above.* Fringe a strip of linen or linen-blend fabric and wrap it loosely around the tumbler. Hold the fabric in place with raffia.

Birds roosting in a stalk of maize make up the motif appliquéd to the table runner, *opposite.* You can adjust the size of the runner to fit your own table. Or use this design to make a seasonal banner for your front door or wall.

Reduce the birds-in-maize motif from the runner on page 61 for the stenciled design, *opposite.* Add touches of embroidery to the birds, and outline the stalk's tassel with chain stitches.

The embroidered dove with olive branch, *opposite,* is a Southwestern version of this universal symbol of peace. Use wool yarn and simple stitches for this design.

To accent these framed pieces or any other picture or photograph, marbleize the mats. Lightly dab paint onto the mats with a sponge to duplicate the pattern and texture of turquoise.

The folk art rocking toys, *above right,* can double as contemporary folk art. Cut out the two major pieces from wood, connect them with dowels, and brush on painted details in quick strokes.

Pick three or four fabrics in soft desert colors for the patchwork pillows, *below right.* Stitch together strips and squares to make the square or rectangular pillow shapes. For a subtle touch of hand quilting, layer the pillow top with batting and a muslin piece, and outline-quilt each fabric shape.

Strip-Pieced Patchwork Quilt

Shown on page 54–55.
Finished size is approximately 44x61 inches.

MATERIALS

Note: Fabrics are 45 inches wide
3¾ yards of purple
2 yards *each* of rust, teal, rose, and pink
½ yard *each* of peach and tan
Quilt batting

INSTRUCTIONS

Note: Use ¼-inch seam allowances throughout. Always sew with right sides facing throughout unless otherwise noted.

CUTTING THE PIECES: Cut purple fabric into two 1⅞-yard lengths. Cut one 24½x65-inch piece from each length for the quilt backing. To simplify cutting, many border pieces are longer than necessary; trim each piece as directed.

From rust, cut:
    Four 1½x67½-inch strips (patchwork panel)
    Two 1¾x67½-inch strips (patchwork panel)
    Two 1x43-inch strips (sides)
    Four 1½x67½-inch strips (binding)

From purple, cut:
    Four 1½x67½-inch strips (patchwork panel)
    Two 1¾x67½-inch strips (patchwork panel)
    Two 1x43-inch strips (center)
    Two 1½x43-inch strips (center)
    Four 2¼x67½-inch strips (border)
    Four 2⅞x67½-inch strips (border)

From teal, cut:
    Four 1½x67½-inch strips (patchwork panel)
    One 1½x43-inch strip (center)
    Two ¾x43-inch strips (center)
    Four 1½x67½-inch strips (border)

color	size
rust	1¾
tan	1½
peach	1½
pink	1½
rose	1½
teal	1½
purple	1½
rust	1½
peach	1½
tan	1½
pink	1½
purple	1½
rust	1½
rose	1½
teal	1½
purple	1¾

ru			
t	ru		
pe	t	ru	
pi	pe	t	
ro	pi	pe	
tl	ro	pi	
pu	tl	ro	
ru	pu	tl	
pe	ru	pu	
t	pe	ru	
pi	t	pe	
pu	pi	t	
ru	pu	pi	
ro	ru	pu	
tl	ro	ru	
pu	tl	ro	
	pu	tl	
		pu	

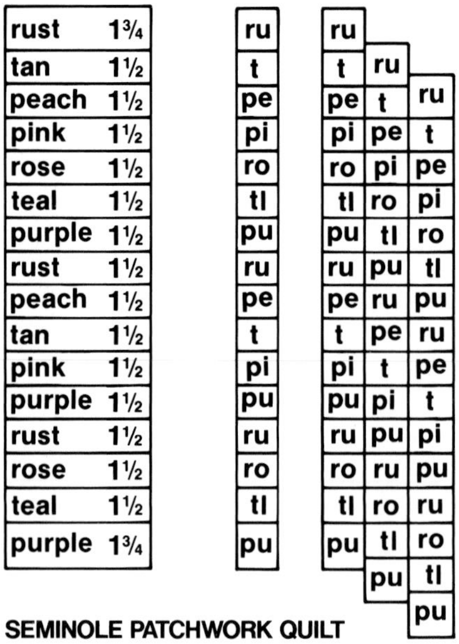

SEMINOLE PATCHWORK QUILT

Four 2¼x67½-inch strips (border)
Four ¾x67½-inch strips (border)

From rose, cut:
    Four 1½x67½-inch strips (patchwork panel)
    Two 1x43-inch strips (center)
    Four 1¼x67½-inch strips (border)
    Four 1½x67½-inch strips (border)
    Four ¾x67½-inch strips (border)

From pink, cut:
    Four 1½x67½-inch strips (patchwork panel)
    Four 1½x67½-inch strips (border)
    Four ¾x67½-inch strips (border)

From peach and tan, cut:
    Six 1½x45-inch strips (patchwork panel)

PIECING THE STRIPS: Sew strips together lengthwise in the order shown in chart, *above,* to make one large, long piece. Press all seams to one direction. *Note:* To join lengths of same-color strips, simply overlap ends and continue sewing.

Cut across pieces to make 1½-inch strips. See diagram, *above,* for detail. Discard the strips where overlapping occurred. Sew strips together, sliding down one row with each strip; continue until all pieces have been used. See diagram, *left,* for detail. Press seam allowances to one side.

Trim off points on outer edges. Cut across piece to make bottom and top edges at right angles with sides. *Note:* Finished block will be one large rectangle with colors running in straight lines and squares running diagonally. See photograph on page 54.

FOR THE BACKING: Sew together the purple backing pieces, lengthwise. Cut batting to same size; baste batting to wrong side of backing.

ASSEMBLY: For the quilt's center stripes, pin a 1½-inch teal strip lengthwise down the center of the batting, placing the end 11 inches from the top. Machine-baste around the strip ⅛ inch from raw edges, through all thicknesses.

Place one 1-inch rose strip atop teal strip, right sides together and aligning raw edges. Sew outer edge of rose strip through all layers, leaving other edge free. Repeat for second rose strip on other long side of teal strip. Open out the rose strips; pin each flat to backing, encasing the raw edges of the teal. Repeat with 1-inch purple, ¾-inch teal, and 1½-inch purple strips.

Cut the panel into two 43-inch lengths. Place over outer purple strip and sew as for center strips. The rust edges should align with the center purple strips. Sew the 1x43-inch rust strips to opposite sides of the center panel along the purple patchwork pieces.

For borders, piece and sew the strips as for center strips, sewing side (long) borders first, then upper and lower borders. Trim lengths of border strips after each is stitched in place. Upper and lower borders will cross and butt side borders at right angles. Color sequence for border strips is as follows: 1½-inch pink, 1¼-inch rose, ¾-inch pink, 1½-inch rose, 1½-inch teal, ¾-inch rose, 2¼-inch teal, 2¼-inch purple, ¾-inch teal, and 2⅞-inch purple.

After attaching the borders, baste outer purple edges in place, using ⅛-inch seams. Bind the edges with rust fabric.

To prevent patchwork strips from bagging, invisibly hand-tack centers of the pieced rows to the backing and batting.

Serape Stockings
Shown on page 54.

MATERIALS
Serape *or* ⅜ yard of striped wool fabric
⅜ yard *each* of muslin and lightweight quilt batting
Thread
Water-erasable marker

INSTRUCTIONS
Enlarge pattern on page 82. Fold serape or fabric in half, aligning strips. Lay pattern atop the serape or striped fabric so that the stripes run diagonally across the stocking. Trace the outline. Adding ½-inch seam allowances, cut out stocking front and back.

Cut muslin and batting to 18x22 inches. Layer muslin, batting, and stocking front; baste. Machine-quilt along stripes, every 1½–2½ inches. Trim excess batting and muslin.

Place stocking front and back right sides together; stitch around, leaving top open. Clip curves and turn stocking.

Cut a cuff from fringed edge of serape or from wool fabric to fit around stocking top. Sew short ends of cuff together to form tube. Keeping cuff seam to back of stocking, pin right side of cuff to wrong side of top edge of stocking. Sew along top edge. Trim seams to reduce bulk; turn cuff to right side.

Painted Bead Necklaces
Shown on page 54.

MATERIALS
Strands of ⅝-inch-diameter wooden beads
Chrome spray paint (available at auto supply stores)
Light and dark turquoise paint
Sponge

INSTRUCTIONS
Separate the beads into 32- to 40-inch lengths, if necessary. Tie ends securely.

For silver beads, spray paint with chrome paint.

For turquoise beads, paint the beads first with the dark turquoise paint; let dry. Then, sponge with light turquoise paint, letting some of the dark paint show through.

Felt Doll and Angel Ornament
Shown on pages 58–59.
Finished sizes of dolls are approximately 10 and 20 inches high.

MATERIALS
For small doll (with angel wings)
Synthetic felt: 2 squares tan (skin), 1 square of any color (dress)
12x12-inch piece of lightweight fusible webbing
10 yards of 1/16-inch-wide black satin ribbon (hair)
1½ yards of ¼-inch-wide satin ribbon to match dress
4¼x10-inch piece of 14-count waste canvas
8x10-inch piece of medium-weight white paper (wings)
Crafts knife

For large doll
Synthetic felt: ¾ yard of tan for skin, ½ yard of any color (dress)
¾ yard of lightweight fusible webbing
20 yards of 1/16-inch-wide black satin ribbon (hair)
¼ yard of ½-inch-wide satin ribbon to match dress
8½x20-inch piece of 14-count waste canvas

For both
Small piece of red synthetic felt (cheeks)
Two beads or buttons (eyes)
6-ply embroidery floss in the following colors: 3 skeins of white plus small amounts of black and red
Scrap of eyelet lace (bodice)
Pinking shears; leather needle
Cardboard; crafts glue
Polyester fiberfill
Water-erasable marker

INSTRUCTIONS
Patterns on page 66 are full size for smaller ornament. For larger doll, draw a 1-inch grid over pattern pieces; transfer pattern pieces onto a 2-inch grid. Or have the pattern enlarged 200 percent at a quick-print shop. Assembly instructions for doll and angel are identical, except that doll does not have wings; any references to materials or specific instructions for the larger doll appear in parentheses.

Press fusible webbing to wrong side of tan felt. Using water-erasable marker, transfer two body outlines to felt; add hair and facial features to one shape. Do not cut out the pieces.

FACE: Embroider the mouth with stem stitches using 6 plies of black floss. Cut two cheeks from red felt; hand-appliqué in place using 6 plies of red floss. Sew eyes in place.
continued

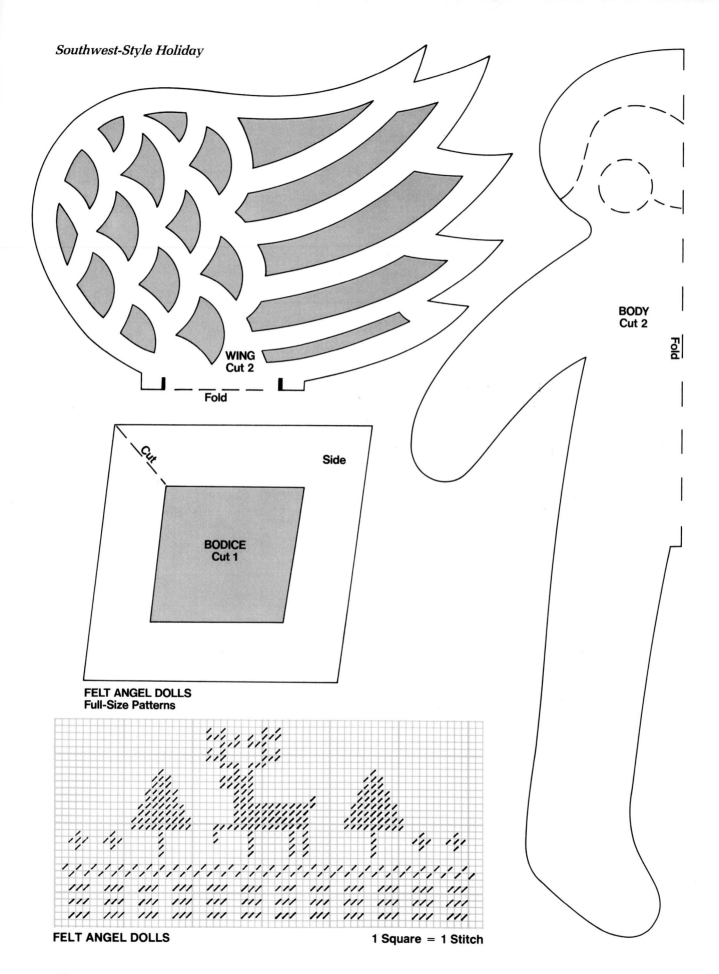

WING
Cut 2

Fold

BODY
Cut 2

Fold

Cut

Side

BODICE
Cut 1

FELT ANGEL DOLLS
Full-Size Patterns

FELT ANGEL DOLLS

1 Square = 1 Stitch

HAIR: Using 24-inch lengths of narrow black ribbon and leather needle, embroider hair using satin stitches. *Note:* Make sure ribbon does not twist and that the stitches are close enough to cover felt. Embroider both back and front of head, but not ponytails.

BODY: Pin front to back with wrong sides together. Machine-stitch around outer edge of body, stitching just outside ribbon work. Cut with pinking shears, being careful not to cut ribbon. Clip corners with regular scissors.

Make a 2-inch-long slit in body back. Firmly stuff through opening. Slip-stitch closed.

Secure a doubled strand of thread at waist with single stitch. Wrap thread around waist tightly to make waistline.

DRESS: For skirt, cut pieces of felt to match waste canvas; baste canvas to felt. Referring to chart, *opposite,* work the design over waste canvas. Work a half cross-stitch for every symbol on the chart using 6 plies of white floss over one (two) threads of canvas. Remove waste canvas. Blanket-stitch along hem and back edges.

Sew eight ¼-inch (½-inch) tucks at waist to fit skirt to waistline. Sew skirt to doll, overlapping in back.

Cut bodice from felt. Blanket-stitch along all edges. Glue eyelet in place on back of bodice front. Glue bodice in place. (See photograph on page 55.)

PONYTAILS: Wrap narrow black ribbon around 1-inch-wide (2-inch-wide) piece of cardboard 10 times; sew into bundle at base. Repeat for second ponytail. Sew or glue into place. Tie colored ribbon in single knot; trim ends. Glue ribbon under ponytails.

WINGS: Add wings to small doll only. Cut piece from white paper; cut out shaded sections with crafts knife. Thread 32-inch colored ribbons through slots and tie in place. Tie wings to back of angel.

Tin and Wood Wreath

Shown on page 57.
Finished diameter is 19 inches.

MATERIALS
20x20-inch piece of ¾-inch plywood
Scraps of sheet aluminum (available at crafts supply stores)
Small nails or tacks
Upholstery tacks
Tin snips; hammer
Black paint; felt-tip marker

INSTRUCTIONS
For pattern, draw a 19-inch circle; center a 5-inch-diameter circle inside. Make gentle scallops along outer edges of circle; see photograph on page 57. Cut wreath from plywood. Sand all edges lightly.

To make leaf pattern, draw a 3½-inch-long flattened, pointed oval shape on paper; see photograph on page 57. Trace pattern onto aluminum and cut out approximately 50 leaves.

Arrange leaves onto plywood circle, overlapping tips slightly. Tack tips of leaves in place.

Press upholstery tacks in inner and outer edges of wreath. Coat entire surface with black paint; wipe away excess paint from metal surfaces with rag before paint dries.

Wire Candle Holders

Shown on page 57.

MATERIALS
24-inch lengths of ³⁄₃₂-inch-diameter wire
2-inch-diameter wooden balls
6-inch length of ¾-inch-diameter wooden dowel
Drill; wire cutters
Silver spray paint; glue
Clear plastic pushpins

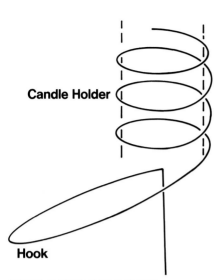

Candle Holder

Hook

WIRE CANDLE HOLDERS

INSTRUCTIONS
Wrap wire around dowel three or four times to shape candle cup. To form hanging loop, extend wire on last wrap; see diagram, *above.*

Drill each ball to fit wire snugly. Spray paint beads silver; let dry.

Clip wires to differing desired lengths. Insert wire through beads and glue beads in place as desired.

Secure holder to window or ledge with pushpin through loop. Insert and adjust lower wire and beads as necessary. *Note:* Do not leave lighted candles unattended.

Soft-Sculpture Nativity

Shown on page 56.

MATERIALS
½ yard of fabric for each adult figure
⅛ yard *each* of muslin and black fabric
6x36-inch remnant for each shawl
8x36-inch remnant linen for infant
Polyester fiberfill; sand *or* beans
Two small plastic bags
Thread; florist's wire
Cardboard
Scraps of fusible webbing
Assorted beads; twine

continued

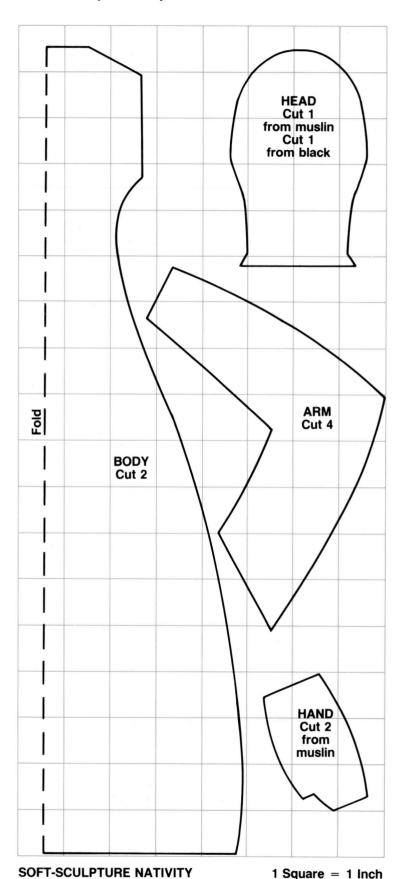

SOFT-SCULPTURE NATIVITY　　　　**1 Square = 1 Inch**

INSTRUCTIONS

Enlarge patterns, *left*, and cut out pieces in appropriate fabrics. Pattern pieces include seam allowances. Stitch with right sides facing.

ADULT FIGURES: Sew hand to end of each arm, right sides together; press. Sew arms to body front at shoulders; press. Sew muslin head to neckline of body front; press. Repeat for back of figure, substituting black head for muslin head.

Sew body front to back, leaving bottom open. Clip curves and turn. Stuff firmly with fiberfill. Embed small bag of sand or beans in base.

Cut a 5-inch-diameter cardboard circle and a 6-inch-diameter fabric circle. Fuse fabric to cardboard, following manufacturer's instructions. Sew long running stitches around seam allowance; pull ends to gather fabric tightly around cardboard. Tie ends securely. Slip-stitch base to bottom of doll, easing as necessary.

Fray all ends of shawl fabric; drape around figure using pins or twine to hold securely in place.

String beads onto wire and insert into head of figure to form halo.

INFANT: Wrap bead in center of 5x25-inch strip of muslin; secure with wire. Fold muslin "tail" several times to form body.

Fray all ends of linen. Fold lengthwise tuck in linen. Tie linen in overhand knot, leaving loop in end for bead. Place muslin-covered bead in loop of knot; tuck body into knot. String beads onto wire and loop into halo, leaving long ends. Place halo on head; tuck wire ends behind head and secure with tape. Pin or stitch infant into place.

Drum Ornaments

Shown on page 58.

MATERIALS

Large-size tuna cans
Red self-adhesive vinyl
Chamois; string; crafts knife
Large needle
Red and black stencil paint
Stencil brushes; stencil material

INSTRUCTIONS

Empty cans and remove bottoms. Wash thoroughly and remove any labels. Cut strips of self-adhesive vinyl and adhere to sides of each can.

Cut two chamois circles approximately ¾ inch larger than top of can. Draw 1½-inch-diameter circle on paper. Divide circle with zigzag line; cut stencil for each half of circle. Stencil design onto center of chamois with red and black paints.

With pencil, mark odd number of equidistant spots around chamois ¼ inch from outer edges of chamois circles. Pierce chamois with knife at dots.

Place circles on top and bottom of can. Thread string through one hole in top chamois and knot. Thread through bottom hole. Continue lacing around can, threading through *every other hole*, until you reach the beginning knot. Repeat process by lacing into remaining holes; tie off after all holes are laced.

Tie 8-inch strings to drum lacings to hang.

Rag Ball Ornaments

Shown on pages 58–59.

MATERIALS
3-inch-diameter plastic foam balls
Large box of straight pins
Scissors
Fabric and ribbon scraps

INSTRUCTIONS

Divide fabric and ribbon into color groups; use one color group for each ornament. For interest, try to include as much diversity as possible within each ornament by using a variety of scraps in different textures and weights, such as socks, sweaters, knits, laces, ribbons, novelty trim, clothing labels, netting, tulle, felt, string, twine, prints, solids, and plaids.

Cut fabrics into 1-inch squares and ribbons and strings into 1-inch lengths. A shoe box filled with snippets will cover one ornament.

Fold each square in half diagonally, then in half again to form 4-layer triangle. Insert pin at folded point of triangle and stick into foam ball. To attach ribbon, insert pin at center of strip, fold in half, and stick into foam ball. Begin at any point and cover ball densely with materials. Work in one basic direction, and fluff out fabrics and ribbons as you work.

Add a ribbon or string as hanging loop.

Birds-in-Maize Table Runner

Shown on page 61.
Finished size is approximately 26x95 inches.

MATERIALS
2¾ yards of 54-inch-wide linen
1 yard of green fabric
Scraps of six print and solid fabrics
Threads to match fabrics
2 yards of fusible webbing
Scraps of black and gold 3-ply Persian yarn

INSTRUCTIONS

Note: Dimensions of table runner may be altered to fit your table by using desired length of fabric and enlarging design to fit that length and width.

Cut linen to size. Finish all edges with a ¼-inch rolled hem. Press and set aside.

Enlarge cornstalk and bird pattern on page 72, reversing and tracing pattern to complete. Cut two cornstalks from green fabric and 12 birds from scraps.

Lay runner across table and position cornstalks accordingly. Fuse to runner. Fuse the birds to cornstalks as indicated on pattern. Machine-zigzag around each shape with matching threads.

Using chain stitches, embroider corn tassels with gold yarn. Outline-stitch bird feet with black yarn.

Bird Ornaments

Shown on page 60.

MATERIALS
⅛ yard of fabric
Scrap of cotton quilt batting
Polyester fiberfill
Water-erasable marker
Thread

INSTRUCTIONS

Note: All pattern pieces include ¼-inch seam allowances. Transfer full-size patterns on page 70 to paper for master patterns.

Cut out all pieces from fabric. Mark all dots and dotted lines on right sides of fabric with water-erasable marker.

Sew bodies together along head and back pieces between dots, right sides together. Clip curves.

Sew underbody to body, matching dot and leaving tail end open. Clip curves and turn to right side. Baste under raw edges of tail end of underbody along seam allowances. Stuff bird firmly with polyester fiberfill.

Cut quilt batting to fit one tail section and two wings. Baste batting to wrong side of one tail section. With right sides together, sew tail sections together, leaving an opening for turning. Clip curves; turn right side out. Slip-stitch opening closed; lightly press tail. Topstitch around tail, ¼ inch from edge.

Insert tail into opening of body. *Note:* Top of opening should align with topstitching; bottom of opening should align with dotted line on tail. Slip-stitch securely in place.

Baste quilt batting to wrong side of one wing. With right sides together, sew two wing pieces together, leaving an opening for turning. Clip curves; turn. Slip-stitch opening closed and press lightly. Topstitch along dotted lines. Repeat for second wing.

Pin wings to body, matching Xs. Slip-stitch in place along dotted line, allowing remainder of the wing to hang free.

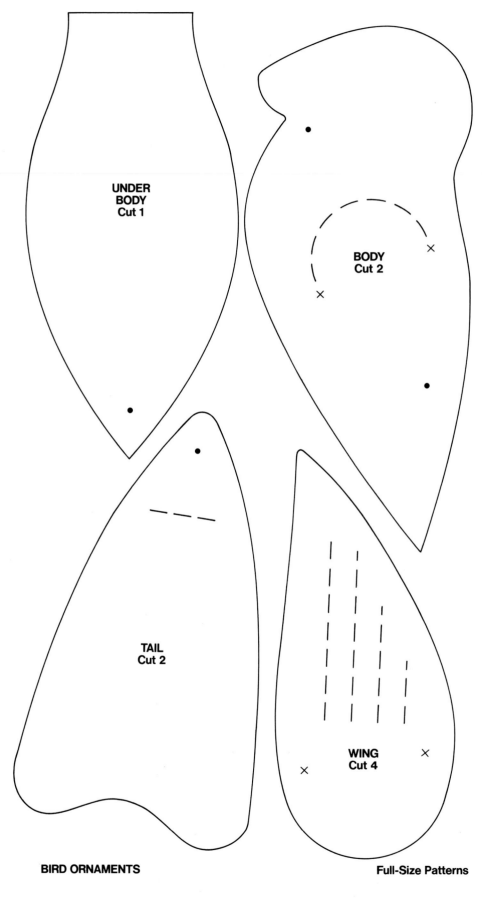

BIRD ORNAMENTS

UNDER
BODY
Cut 1

BODY
Cut 2

TAIL
Cut 2

WING
Cut 4

Full-Size Patterns

Patchwork Pillows

Shown on page 63.
Pillows are approximately 16x16
and 16x20 inches.

MATERIALS

Small amounts of fabrics in the
  following colors: Coral, sand,
  rust, teal, sage green, purple,
  and peach
1 yard of fabric for piping and
  backing
Piping cord
½ yard of muslin
½ yard of quilt batting
Polyester fiberfill; thread

INSTRUCTIONS

Refer to the pillow diagrams, *opposite,* and the photograph on page
63 to determine the color placement
and to arrange the pieces.

For pattern pieces, make a 4x4-
inch and an 8x8-inch cardboard or
plastic template. Make 4x8-inch,
4x12-inch, and 4x16-inch templates.
Templates are finished size; add ¼-
inch seam allowances before cutting pieces from fabric.

Cut out pieces and lay out pillow
fronts. Using ¼-inch seams, stitch
each piece together. Stitch sections
into rows whenever possible, and
then stitch the rows together.

Press seams toward one side.

Cut muslin and batting to fit pillow front. Baste batting to muslin;
pin wrong side of pillow front to batting. Quilt ¼ inch inside all stitching
lines, stitching through all thicknesses.

Cut pillow back from fabric. Cover cord with piping and stitch to pillow front. Place pillow front and
back right sides together. Stitch
along piping line, leaving an opening
for turning. Turn, stuff, and slip-
stitch closed.

A

3	2	1
2	4	
4	1	3

B

1	2
3	4
4	3
2	

**PATCHWORK
PILLOWS**

	A	B		A	B
1.	Coral	Sand	3.	Sand	Sage
2.	Rust	Teal	4.	Purple	Peach

Folk Art
Rocking Toys
Shown on page 63.

MATERIALS
15-inch length of 1x10 (dove)
15-inch length of 1x12 (rooster)
26-inch length of 2x8 (bases)
⅜-inch-diameter dowels (legs)
⅜-inch drill bit
Drill
Wood glue
Semigloss latex *or* acrylic paints
Polyurethane varnish

INSTRUCTIONS
Enlarge patterns, *right,* and transfer to wood pieces. Cut out each bird shape and two bases with jigsaw or bandsaw. Sand the edges and surfaces lightly.

Drill holes for legs on birds as marked on pattern. Drill ¾-inch-deep holes into tops of bases as indicated on pattern.

continued

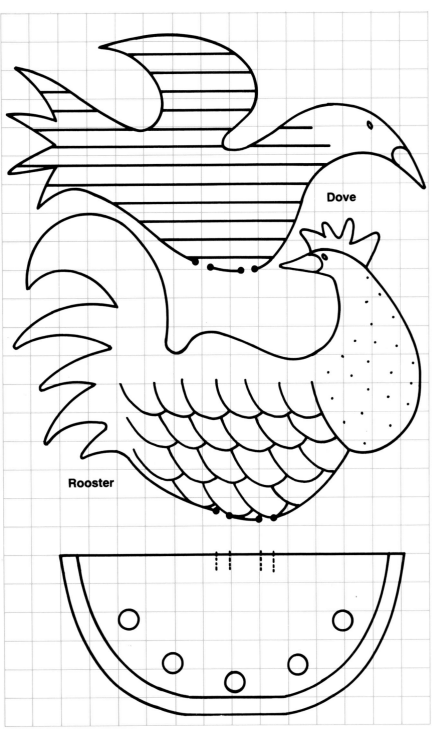

FOLK ART ROCKING TOYS
Dove
Rooster

1 Square = 1 Inch

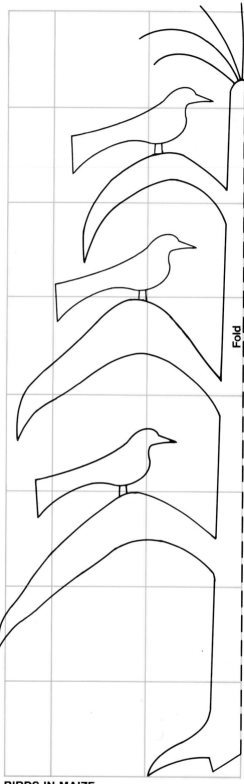

BIRDS IN MAIZE
Table Runner: 1 Square = 4 Inches
Stencils: Full-Size Pattern

Cut dowels into 3-inch lengths, two for each bird.

Paint the toys as desired, using photograph on page 63 for ideas. Use free, loose painting strokes to duplicate the look of the toys shown.

Insert legs into birds; glue in place. Secure legs to bases.

Seal with two coats of polyurethane varnish, sanding lightly between coats.

Marbleized Picture Mats

Shown on page 62.

MATERIALS

White heavy cardboard picture mats
Acrylic paints: White, wedgwood green, colonial blue, walnut brown, copen blue, phthalo blue
Clear acrylic spray
1-inch-wide foam brush
Cosmetic sponge
Soft-bristled brush
Disposable pie tin

INSTRUCTIONS

Pour a small amount of wedgwood green into pie tin. Dab over mat in thin blotchy coat using cosmetic sponge.

Working quickly, whisk and stipple surface with bristled brush.

Add small amount of colonial blue to pie tin. Sponge on in a few areas to darken the green. Blend edges with bristled brush.

Sponge on a few light streaks of walnut; blend with sponge or brush.

Sponge on copen blue in widely spaced large blotches and blend; darken blotches with phthalo blue.

When paint is dry, seal with two coats of acrylic spray.

Birds-in-Maize Stencil

Shown on page 62.
Design is about 6x8 inches.

MATERIALS

14x14-inch piece of tightly woven muslin
Stencil paints (suitable for stenciling on fabric)
Stencil brushes
Stencil material
Crafts knife
Gold and black embroidery floss

INSTRUCTIONS

Using full-size pattern, *left,* cut a stencil of cornstalk and an individual bird.

Stencil cornstalk onto muslin in color desired. Add a bird to each stalk. When paint is dry, heat-set on wrong side with iron.

Embroider corn tassels with chain stitches using gold floss. Add bird legs with black long stitches. If desired, add texture and design to birds by using various colors of embroidery floss with French knots and straight stitches.

Frame as desired.

Bird Stitchery

Shown on page 62.

MATERIALS

10x10-inch piece of linen
Brown and black crewel yarn
Embroidery needle
Water-erasable marker
Tracing paper

INSTRUCTIONS

Draw a 7⅝-inch-diameter circle on linen. Center and transfer pattern, *opposite,* to the fabric.

Using single ply of black yarn, outline-stitch entire design except wings, tail, beak, eye, and upper legs. Using single ply of brown yarn, fill in body (shaded light gray on pattern) with chain stitches. Satin-stitch remainder of design with black yarn.

Press and frame as desired.

BIRD STITCHERY

Full-Size Pattern

Christmas at the Shore

A trip to the shore for Christmas is a favorite getaway for many families. Our holiday visit to a woodland retreat includes home decorating ideas using natural materials and gift suggestions for the whole family.

The striking tree, *right,* is a collector's delight. It's trimmed with shells, sand dollars, starfish, and a garland of bobbers strung on fishing line. Substitute nature's collectibles from your region to trim your own tree.

Reminiscent of the hardy woolens made for the outdoors, the stocking, *left,* is accented with a machine-quilted diagonal grid. Make the cuff from a coordinating wool plaid, and add piping for the finishing touch.

For sailors of any expertise, the toy boat, *left,* is a seaworthy craft you can make in a twinkling. Rough-cut the hull from a 2x4 scrap, and fit the boat with a mast and a crossarm cut from dowels.

Instructions for the projects in this chapter begin on page 82.

Evergreen trees and antlered deer, recurring motifs in crafts from forestlands, are especially appropriate at Christmas. This collection of projects is based on one design combining these figures.

The pine tree and stag motif is worked in filet crochet for the pillow top and window ornament, *left.* The crocheted panel, which you can work in any color of thread, can be framed between two sheets of clear acrylic or stitched to a ruffled pillow.

Embroidered in cross-stitch, the same design is ideal for welcoming samplers (in red or green), *above right,* or repeated across the bottom edges of place mats, *below right.* For the samplers, stitch over two threads, except for the word "Greetings," which is stitched over one thread. Consider substituting a family name or similar sentiment. Stitch five repeats of the motif over one thread of fabric for the generously sized place mats.

For cozy comfort, knit the fisherman-style afghan, *left* and *below right.* This throw is made of panels textured with the familiar cable and traditional allover patterns that are the hallmark of this popular knitting style.

For a woodlands welcome, fasten an arrangement of assorted evergreen boughs to your front door, *above left.* Trim the branches with a bright grosgrain ribbon bow, a well-used fishing creel, and two or three lures.

Cleverly crafted wooden ornaments that resemble fish lures are mixed with quick-and-easy trims on the tree, *right.*

For starters, wrap plastic foam balls with rug yarn for the striped ornaments. The colors and patterns for these, *right* and *below left,* are based on those found on awnings, but you can make them any style you choose.

Kids can help make the deeply notched stars, cut from colored cardboard. Begin with six- to eight-inch squares of cardboard, and freehand-cut narrow, slightly irregular points. Then just set the stars on the branches. If your tree has bushy needles and branches, hang the stars from loops of ribbon or yarn.

Collect a basketful of natural materials for the miniature wreaths, including pinecones, shells, and dried pods. Arrange and glue them to wreath bases cut from hardboard.

Constructing the fish lure ornaments, *right* and *below left,* is just the beginning. The fun begins when you paint bright swirls, circles, zigzags, and dots on the sides of the lures.

The handsome hooked rug, *opposite,* is a five-star example of how leftover woolen fabric can be put to good use. This rug can be made any size to take the center spot in an entry, to fit beside a bed or sofa, or to use anywhere else in the house. To duplicate the primitive appeal of this project, freehand-draw the stars on the rug backing, and don't worry about crooked lines or uneven points.

Pinecones and seashells—plentiful materials that are easy to collect—are used together for the spectacular wreath, *below.* A dried starfish, framed by five slender pinecones and trimmed with a twine bow, is the focal point. Position the materials atop a tiered wreath form (available at crafts supply stores) and glue them to the form in an orderly arrangement.

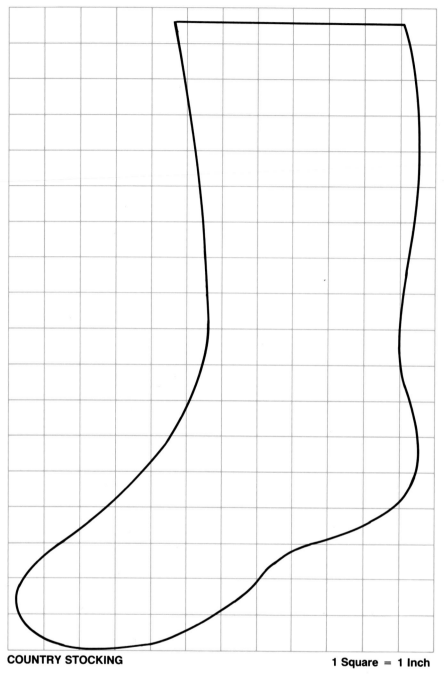

COUNTRY STOCKING

1 Square = 1 Inch

Country Stocking

Shown on page 74.
Finished height is 17½ inches.

MATERIALS
⅜ yard of wool fabric (stocking)
⅜ yard of muslin (lining)
½ yard of plaid fabric
1½ yards and ½ yard of piping in
    different colors
⅜ yard of lightweight quilt batting
Water-erasable marker

INSTRUCTIONS
Enlarge pattern, *left;* cut out paper pattern. Mark one shape (front) on wool; turn pattern over and mark another shape (back). Do not cut out pieces.

Layer wool, batting, and muslin; baste layers. Using 1-inch-wide masking tape to create guidelines on wool and using contrasting thread, machine-quilt stocking with 1-inch grid positioned on the diagonal.

Complete as directed for Serape Stocking on page 65, substituting quilted wool fabric for serape and bias-cut plaid cuff for fringed edge of serape.

Pipe edges of stocking (except top edges) and bottom edge of cuff.

Toy Boat

Shown on page 74.
Finished size of hull is 3⅝x6⅛ inches.

MATERIALS
8-inch length of pine 2x4
4 inches of ⅝-inch dowel
3 inches of ¼-inch dowel
Drill; drill bits
Sandpaper; rasp; glue
Black fine-tipped marker
Wood sealer;
Gloss polyurethane varnish

INSTRUCTIONS
Trace top and side from full-size patterns, *opposite,* onto 2x4; cut out.

Use a rasp to shape, round, and rough-finish hull. Drill hole for mast as indicated. Sand hull.

Drill a ¼-inch-diameter hole in the ⅝-inch-diameter dowel, ½ inch

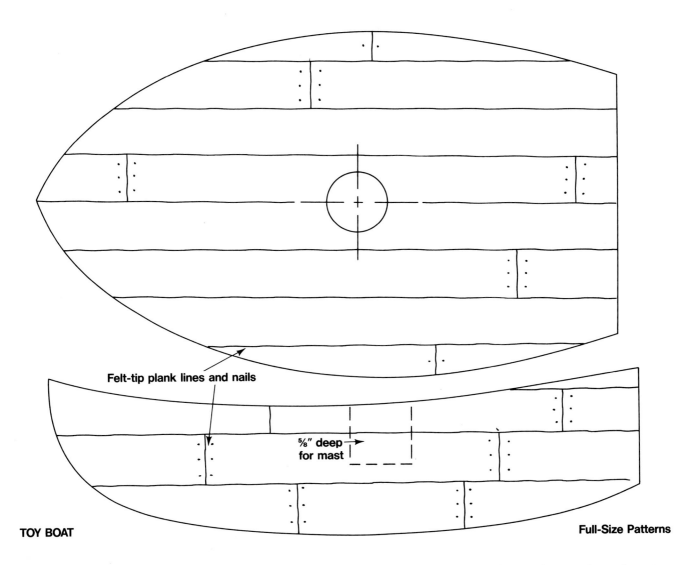

Felt-tip plank lines and nails

⅝" deep
for mast

TOY BOAT

Full-Size Patterns

from top; insert 3-inch-long ¼-inch dowel crossarm here.

Varnish; add details (see pattern) with marker. Varnish again.

Stag and Pine Tree Sampler

Shown on page 77.
Design is 78x132 stitches.
Stitchery is 8¾x14¾ inches.

MATERIALS

18x24-inch piece of camel 18-count Davosa cloth
DMC embroidery floss: 4 skeins red (304) *or* green (367)
Graph paper
Tapestry needle; embroidery hoop

INSTRUCTIONS

Note: The chart on pages 84 and 85 indicates stitches marked with Xs and Os; differentiation regarding these symbols is made in the directions for completing the accompanying Stag and Pine Tree projects in this chapter. For this project, disregard the red lines.

To complete this stitchery, transfer both symbols (Xs and Os) to graph paper. Stitch the word "Greetings" directly from the printed page, if desired, or chart it separately.

Measure 5 inches from top of fabric and 5 inches from left edge; begin upper-left corner of border here.

Use three plies of floss and work the stitches over two threads of fabric, *except* for "Greetings."

Baste area indicated by shading on stitchery pattern. Center "Greet-

ings" within box and stitch, using two plies of floss over one thread.

Frame the stitchery as desired.

Stag and Pine Tree Place Mats

Shown on page 77.
Finished size is approximately 14½x19½ inches.

MATERIALS

For each place mat

18x24-inch piece of camel 18-count Davosa cloth
DMC embroidery floss: 5 skeins red (304) *or* green (367)
Graph paper
Embroidery hoop; tapestry needle
continued

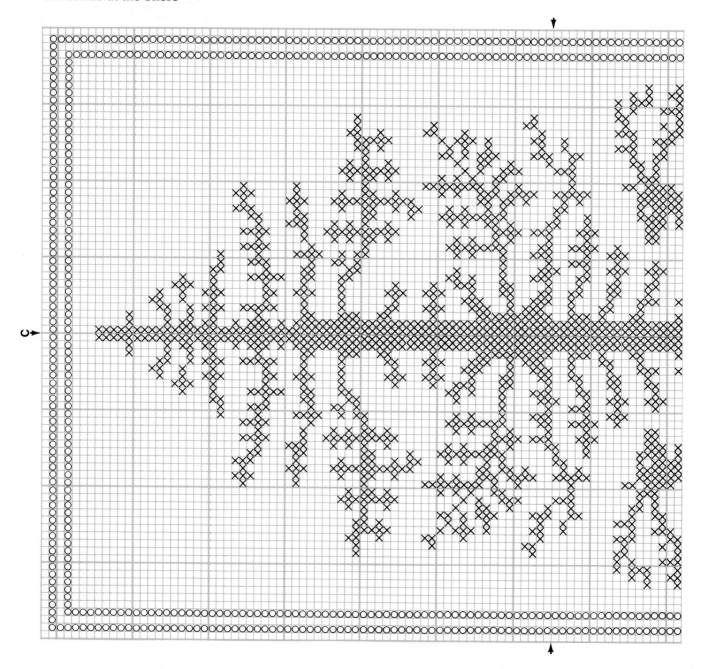

CROCHET ABBREVIATIONS

beg .... begin(ning)
ch .... chain
dc .... double crochet
dec .... decrease
dtr .... double treble
grp .... group
hdc .... half-double crochet
inc .... increase

lp(s) .... loop(s)
pat .... pattern
rem .... remaining
rep .... repeat
rnd .... round
sc .... single crochet
sk .... skip
sl st .... slip stitch

sp .... space
st(s) .... stitch(es)
tog .... together
trc .... treble crochet
yo .... yarn over
*....repeat from * as indicated
( ).......... repeat between ( ) as
indicated

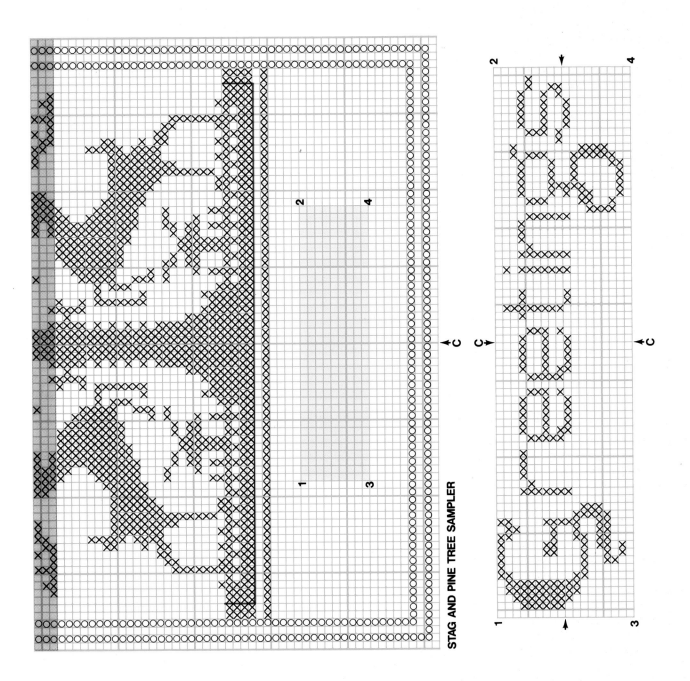

STAG AND PINE TREE SAMPLER

KNITTING ABBREVIATIONS

beg .... begin(ning)	pat .... pattern	st st .... stockinette stitch
dec .... decrease	psso .... pass sl st over	tog .... together
dp .... double-pointed	rem .... remaining	yo .... yarn over
grp .... group	rep .... repeat	*....repeat from * as indicated
inc ....increase	rnd .... round	( ) .... repeat between ( ) as
k .... knit	sk .... skip	indicated
lp(s) .... loop(s)	sl st .... slip stitch	[ ] .... repeat between [ ] as
p .... purl	st(s) .... stitch(es)	indicated

85

INSTRUCTIONS

Note: The chart on pages 84 and 85 indicates stitches marked with Xs and Os; disregard all stitches marked with Os for this project. For the place mats, transfer to graph paper all the symbols above the red line on the pattern as far to the left and right as the red vertical lines; pattern is 68 squares wide across the bottom edge.

Mark vertical centerline of fabric; bind edges with masking tape.

Referring to pattern, begin stitching one motif along centerline, 2 inches above bottom edge of fabric. Use two plies of floss and work the cross-stitches over one thread of fabric.

After center motif is complete, stitch two motifs on either side of center motif.

For border, work a row of cross-stitches, two threads beneath and two threads to either side of motifs. Extend side borders for 14 inches from bottom; complete top border.

Narrowly hem place mat, leaving six threads free between outer edge of border and folded edge.

Filet Crochet Pillow and Window Ornament

Shown on page 76.
Stitchery is 13x21½ inches.

MATERIALS
For both projects
DMC Cébélia crochet cotton, Size 10: 2 balls of desired color
Size 12 steel crochet hook, or size to obtain gauge given
Graph paper; rustproof pins

For window ornament
17x26-inch picture frame
Two sheets of clear, framing-thickness acrylic to fit frame

For pillow
½ yard of fabric
Fabric for ruffle and piping (optional)
Polyester fiberfill

Abbreviations: See page 84.
Gauge: 11 sps = 2 inches;
11 rows = 2 inches.

INSTRUCTIONS
Note: Refer to instructions for Stag and Pine Tree Place Mats, *left*, to create pattern. The pattern is 68 squares wide across bottom edge.

PANEL: Ch 156.
Row 1: Dc in 6th ch from hook, (ch 1, sk 1 ch, dc in next ch) 75 times—76 sps made; ch 4, turn.
Rows 2–3: (Dc in next dc, ch 1) across, dc in third st of turning ch; ch 4, turn.
Rows 4–5: (Dc in next dc, ch 1) 3 times; dc in next dc—4 sps made; (dc in next sp, dc in next dc) 68 times to make 68 bls; end row with 4 sps. Last dc is made in third st of turning ch; ch 4, turn.

Continue working design in this manner, following chart for placement of blocks and sps. All sps consist of 2 dc with ch-1 bet, and all bls have 1 dc in place of the ch-1. There will be 5 rows of plain mesh after the design is finished. Do not fasten off at end of Row 116; ch 1, turn.

EDGING: Working back across Row 116, make 2 sc in beg sp and * 2 sc in each sp to next corner; in corner sp work 4 sc; rep from * around three rem sides, ending with 2 more sc in beg corner; join with sl st to first sc. Fasten off; weave in ends.

FINISHING: Wash the panel, if necessary, in warm soapy water. Rinse thoroughly. Lay out panel on a folded bath towel, aligning stitches and rows until they are straight. Secure in place with rustproof pins and let dry at room temperature.

For window ornament, frame between two sheets of clear acrylic and hang.

For pillow, stitch panel to fabric; trim ½ inch past edges. Make piping and ruffle, if desired, and stitch to pillow front adjacent to panel edge. Place front and back together, and stitch around, using ½-inch seams and leaving an opening for turning. Turn, press, stuff, and slip-stitch opening closed.

Fisherman Afghan

Shown on page 76.
Finished size is approximately 58x70 inches without fringe.

MATERIALS
Coats & Clark Red Heart 4-ply hand-knitting yarn (3½-oz. skeins): 23 skeins eggshell (No. 111)
Size 8 knitting needles, or size to obtain gauge given below
Size H aluminum crochet hook
Double-pointed or cable needle

Abbreviations: See page 85.
Gauge: Over moss st, 5 sts = 1 inch.

INSTRUCTIONS
MOSS AND MOCK CABLE PAT: Pattern is worked over 37 sts.
Rows 1 and 3 (right side): P 1, (k 1, p 1) 4 times; * k 1, k through back lp (tbl), p 2, k 1 tbl, (k 1, p 1) 4 times; k 1; rep from * once again, p 1.
Rows 2, 4, and 6: K 1, * (k 1, p 1) 5 times; k 2, p 1; rep from * once more, ending with (k 1, p 1) 4 times; k 2.
Row 5: P 1, (k 1, p 1) 4 times; k 1, * **yo, k 1, p 2, k 1, pass yo over last 4 sts—mock cable made;** (k 1, p 1) 4 times; k 1; rep from * once more, p 1.
Rep Rows 1–6 for pat.

CABLE PAT: Pattern is worked over 66 sts.
Row 1 (right side): P 5, (k 6, p 4) twice; k 4, **sl 2 to dpn and hold in back of work, k 2, k 2 from dpn—cable 4 back made (C4B); sl 2 to dpn and hold in front of work, k 2, k 2 from dpn—cable 4 front made (C4F);** k 4 (p 4, k 6) twice, p 5.
Rows 2, 4, and 6: K the k sts and p the p sts as they face you.
Row 3: P 5, (k 6, p 4) twice; k 2, C4B, k 4, C4F, k 2 (p 4, k 6) twice; p 5.
Row 5: P 5, **sl 3 sts to dpn and hold in front of work, k 3, k 3 from dpn—cable 6 front made (C6F); p 4, sl 3 sts to dpn and hold in back of work, k 3, k 3 from dpn—cable 6 back made (C6B);** p 4, C4B, k 8, C4F, p 4, C6B, p 4, C6F, p 5.
Rep Rows 1–6 for pat.

MOSS AND MOCK CABLE PANEL: Make two.

Cast on 37 sts. Work Rows 1–6 of pat until total length measures 70 inches, ending with a right-side row. Bind off.

RIGHT EDGE MOSS AND MOCK CABLE PANEL: Make one.

Cast on 41 sts. K 5, place marker, work Row 1 of moss and cable pat over rem 36 sts, omitting first st of pat row. Work even in pat, keeping 5 sts at right edge in garter st (knit every row) and rem sts in moss and mock cable pat, omitting first st of all right-side rows and omitting last st of all wrong-side rows. Work even until total length measures 70 inches, ending with a right-side row. Bind off.

LEFT EDGE MOSS AND MOCK CABLE PANEL: Make one.

Work as for Right Edge Moss and Mock Cable Panel, reversing position of pats, omitting last st of all right-side rows and omitting first st of all wrong-side rows.

CABLE PANEL: Make three.
Cast on 66 sts.
Row 1 (wrong side): Purl.
Next row: Beg cable pat, working until total length measures 70 inches, ending with right-side row.
Bind off.

ASSEMBLY: Arrange panels as follows, beginning at left edge: Left Edge Moss and Mock Cable Panel, (Cable Panel, Moss and Mock Cable Panel) twice; Cable Panel, Right Edge Moss and Mock Cable Panel. With right sides tog, join panels with crochet hook and sl st.

Lay flat, dampen, block, and let dry away from heat.

EDGING: *Row 1:* With right side facing and with crochet hook, work 219 sc evenly across upper edge, keeping work flat; ch 1, turn.

Rows 2 and 3: Work even in sc, ending Row 3 with ch 3, turn.

Row 4 (loop row): * Sk 2 sc, sc in next st, ch 3; rep from * across to within last 3 sts; sk 2 sc, sc in last st—73 ch-3 lps.

Rep edging across other end.

FRINGE: Cut six strands of yarn, each 26 inches long. Fold these strands in half to form a lp. With right side of afghan facing and working along one narrow edge, insert crochet hook from back to front in corner ch-3 lp and draw lp of strands through. Draw loose ends through lp and pull up tightly to form knot.

Rep in each ch-3 lp across. Picking up half the strands of the first knot and the adjacent half of the second knot, make an overhand knot 1 inch below first knot at midpoint bet two upper knots.

* Picking up rem strands of last knot and adjacent half of next knot, make overhand knot as before. Rep from * across. Using 12 strands for each knot, make another row of knots 1 inch below and in line with first row of knots.

Work fringe across opposite narrow end. Trim all fringe ends.

Awning-Stripe Ornaments

Shown on pages 78–79.
Finished diameter is 4 inches.

MATERIALS
4-inch-diameter plastic foam balls
Aunt Lydia's rug yarn: Green, yellow, orange, red, white, and black
White crafts glue
Crafts knife or scissors
Straight pins

INSTRUCTIONS
Coat small portion of ball with glue. Pin length of yarn to glue-coated area, carefully wrapping yarn around pinned end in a spiral.

Continue wrapping, adding glue as you work down the ball. Secure with straight pins as necessary.

To change colors, cut yarn. Begin second color at end of first color; make all subsequent color changes on one side of ball.

Finish half of ball; let dry and remove pins. Repeat for second half.

Add ribbon or yarn hanging loop.

Fish Lure Ornament

Shown on pages 78–79.
Ornament is 10½ inches long.

MATERIALS
Scraps of ½-inch pine and ⅛-inch hardboard
Small screw eyes
Wood glue; sandpaper
Drill
⅛-inch drill bit
Thumbtacks
Self-adhesive dots (slightly smaller than thumbtack heads) in various colors (available at office supply stores)
Red, green, yellow, blue, and black acrylic paints
Artist's brush
Clear acrylic spray
Monofilament *or* narrow ribbon

INSTRUCTIONS
Refer to full-size patterns on page 88. Transfer body piece to pine, and tail and fins to hardboard. Cut out all pieces. Sand all edges and surfaces lightly.

Drill holes for fish fins as indicated by the dots on the pattern. For the side fins, drill holes through body, and for the lower fins, drill holes at each side of body piece at a 45-degree angle.

Insert fins into body holes and tail into slot, securing with glue; let dry. Attach screw eye into body at tail. Paint lure with base coat in desired color; let dry.

With remaining colors, add freehand designs (dots, stripes, zigzags, or swirls) to body. Add brightly colored thumbtacks for eyes. Place self-adhesive dots on tacks for eye centers.

Antique with a wash of diluted black acrylic if desired; let dry. Seal with two coats of acrylic spray, letting acrylic dry between coats.

Add a loop of monofilament or narrow ribbon for hanging.

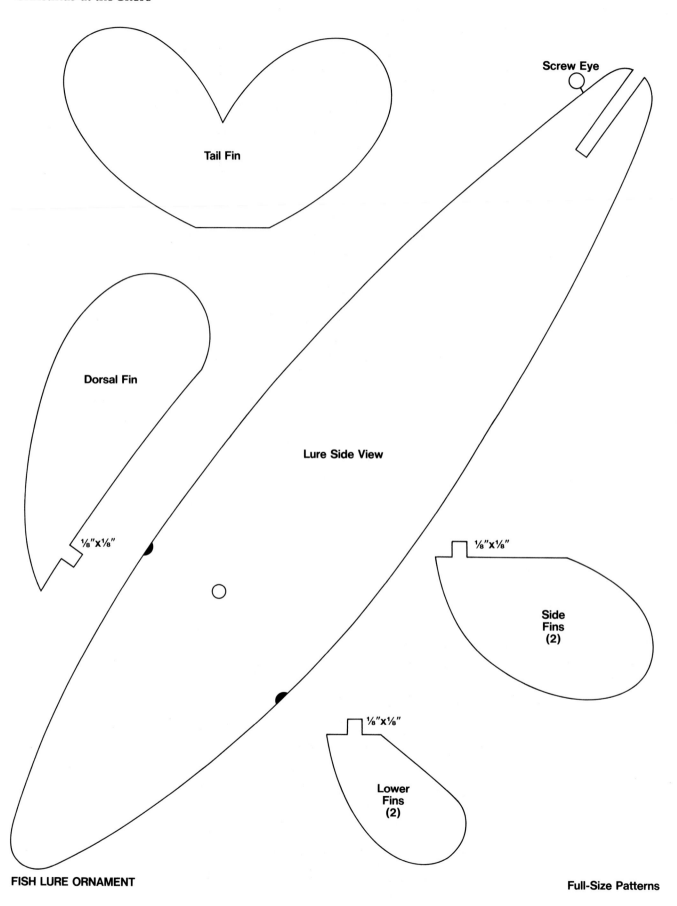

Tail Fin

Dorsal Fin

Lure Side View

Screw Eye

⅛"x⅛"

Side
Fins
(2)

⅛"x⅛"

⅛"x⅛"

Lower
Fins
(2)

FISH LURE ORNAMENT

Full-Size Patterns

Five-Star Rug

Shown on page 80.
Finished size is approximately 40x24 inches.

MATERIALS

46x30-inch piece of burlap
3⅜ yards of rug binding
Rug hook *or* Size 5 *or* 6 crochet hook
Wool scraps
Permanent marker
Masking tape
Large embroidery hoop or frame

INSTRUCTIONS

Draw 40x24-inch rectangle onto burlap. Machine-stitch 1 inch beyond marked line to secure burlap; bind all edges with masking tape.

Draw large star in center of rug and small star in each corner; see photograph on page 80 for positioning ideas.

Cut the wool into strips that are approximately ⅛ inch wide and 12 inches long, taking care to cut along grain. Stretch burlap over frame. Push hook through one mesh of burlap; pull end of wool back through burlap to 1-inch length.

Note: The strip will later be trimmed to match loops. Insert hook into next mesh and pull loop of wool back through burlap to height of approximately ⅛ inch. Continue hooking until strip is used up; pull the end to the front.

Continue with remaining strips, changing colors as needed. Skip holes when pile strains burlap or is too tightly packed. Trim all ends when finished. *Note:* Back of rug should be smooth.

Outline and fill in the stars with the desired colors of wool, then fill in the areas around the stars. If using many colors, work the strips back and forth across the rug in horizontal rows, changing colors randomly and distributing the various colors evenly across the surface.

Trim the edges of the rug and slip-stitch the binding to the burlap.

Shell and Pinecone Wreath

Shown on page 81.

MATERIALS

Pinecones of various sizes and shapes, including 5 long slender ones
18-inch-diameter tiered wire wreath form
11 tun shells of similar size
12 small shells of similar size
Starfish
Twine
Hot-glue gun
Square of light brown felt to fit behind wreath

INSTRUCTIONS

Glue the large pinecones to outer wire circle of the wreath form, positioned slightly up from the bottom edge. Keep the wreath's shape as even as possible and fit pinecones closely together.

Continuing in this manner, glue smaller pinecones to inner circle of wreath; let dry.

For outer edge of wreath, place the five slender pinecones at outer wreath base, with bases of pinecones adjacent and tips pointing outward and slightly upward; glue in place. See photograph on page 81.

Leaving space at the bottom of the wreath for the starfish and twine bow, arrange the tun shells around center of wreath. Position shells uniformly and prominently; glue in place. See photograph. Glue small shells between each of the tun shells.

Glue the starfish in place. Tie the twine into a bow and glue or wire into place.

Fill in any empty spaces with remaining small pinecones.

To protect surface of door or wall, glue a piece of felt to the back of the wreath form.

Miniature Pinecone And Shell Wreath

Shown on page 79.

MATERIALS

5-inch-diameter hardboard circle
Hot-glue gun and clear glue sticks
Small pinecones
Small natural objects such as shells, sponges, dry seaweed, driftwood, starfish, sand dollars, magnolia pods, *or* any other dried native materials

INSTRUCTIONS

Cut 3-inch-diameter circle from center of hardboard to make the wreath base. Glue rings of pinecones around the inner and outer edges of wreath, overlapping as closely as possible. Arrange remaining materials in space between pinecones, filling small spaces with shells and additional pinecones. *Note:* Select one larger, more prominent object as the wreath's focal point and arrange the remaining materials around it for a pleasing and balanced arrangement.

Paper-Punch Luminarias

Shown on page 3.

MATERIALS

Brown paper lunch bags
Paper punch
Sand
Plumber's candles *or* votives

INSTRUCTIONS

With the bag closed, draw three evenly spaced curved lines along both sides. Punch holes along lines, folding bag as needed to allow the punch to reach to the ends of the lines.

Open bag and fill bottom with two inches of sand. Place candle in sand, making sure candle does not touch sides of bag.

Note: For safety, do not burn the candles on windy nights and do not leave lighted candles unattended.

HOLIDAY WORKSHOP

Lively Ornaments to Cross-Stitch

Not only can you trim your tree with these cross-stitch ornaments, you can use them as gift tags on your Christmas packages, too.

These children's designs are stitched using two plies of embroidery floss onto perforated paper—a crisp, stiff paper made especially for cross-stitching and available at crafts and needlework stores.

To make them quick and easy, we left the backgrounds plain and just stitched the details, but you can stitch as much of the background as you want—the beard of Santa, the fur of the bear, the snow of the snowman, for example.

Back the ornaments with red and green felt scraps to make them more sturdy. Trim the felt and leave a narrow edge to outline each shape.

You can even add a bell for the bell's clapper, or a pom-pom to Santa's hat for added embellishments. Then add a ribbon loop for hanging.

Instructions and charts for these seven ornaments are on pages 92 and 93.

Cross-Stitch Ornaments

Shown on pages 90 and 91. Ornaments range from 3½ to 4½ inches high.

MATERIALS

For a set of seven ornaments

Two 9x12-inch sheets of white perforated paper

Bates Anchor embroidery floss: one skein *each* of 024 light pink, 046 red, 044 dark red, 052 dark pink, 098 purple, 0131 blue, 0225 light green, 0227 dark green, 0297 yellow, 0304 orange, 0349 light brown, 0352 dark brown, 0403 black, and 398 gray

Red and green felt

Tapestry needle

Glue; ribbon

Monofilament

INSTRUCTIONS

Full-color charts for the ornaments appear *below* and *opposite.*

Using two plies of floss, work each cross-stitch over one square of the paper.

When stitching, leave about ½ inch between ornaments.

When all cross-stitching is completed, cut out each design, leaving a border of one square of paper around each ornament. Glue each ornament to felt backing, placing glue only on the stitched areas of paper. When the glue has dried, trim the felt ⅛ inch beyond the perforated paper.

If desired, add ribbon bows to tops of ornaments. Add other decorative trims, such as a bell for the bell's clapper, a pom-pom to Santa's hat, and small round beads to the Christmas tree. Loop monofilament through ornaments to hang.

COLOR KEY

- ■ No. 352 Dark brown
- ■ No. 349 Light brown
- ▨ No. 227 Dark green
- ▨ No. 225 Light green
- ■ No. 44 Dark red
- ■ No. 46 Red
- ▨ No. 52 Dark pink
- ▨ No. 24 Light pink
- ■ No. 98 Purple
- ▨ No. 131 Blue
- ▨ No. 304 Orange
- □ No. 297 Yellow
- ▨ No. 398 Gray
- ■ No. 403 Black

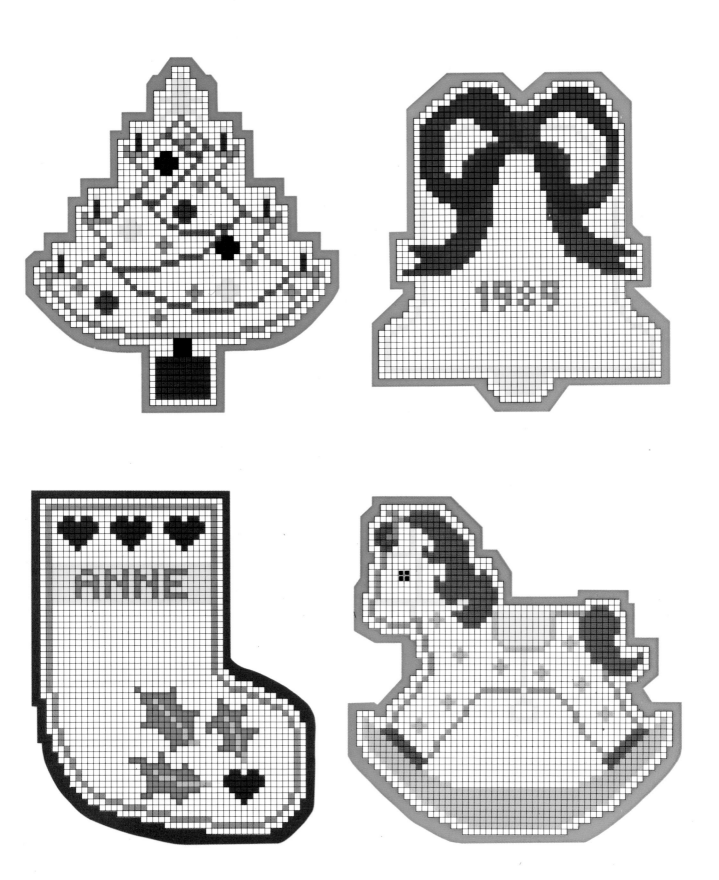

Cheerful Trims to Make from Wood

Cleverly assembled from scraps of softwood, these playful reindeer make winsome ornaments for a holiday centerpiece.

Enlist the whole family to make a herd of these silly-eyed animals with hollylike antlers. Because the wood pieces for the reindeer are cut separately and glued to the main body pieces, they can be assembled into lifelike poses. Kids will love to color them and glue the reindeer's legs so they sit or stand in funny positions.

We painted them with acrylic paints, but kids could easily color them with markers. They even might turn one of the reindeer into Rudolph by gluing a tiny red pom-pom to its nose.

Arrange these critters in a nest of evergreens, holly, and pinecones for a centerpiece that's fun and captivating.

If you are doing a workshop for lots of kids, construct the reindeer from stiff paper and use brads to fasten the legs to the bodies. Then the kids can add ribbon hangers and use their paper deer as tree ornaments.

Instructions and patterns for this project are on pages 96 and 97.

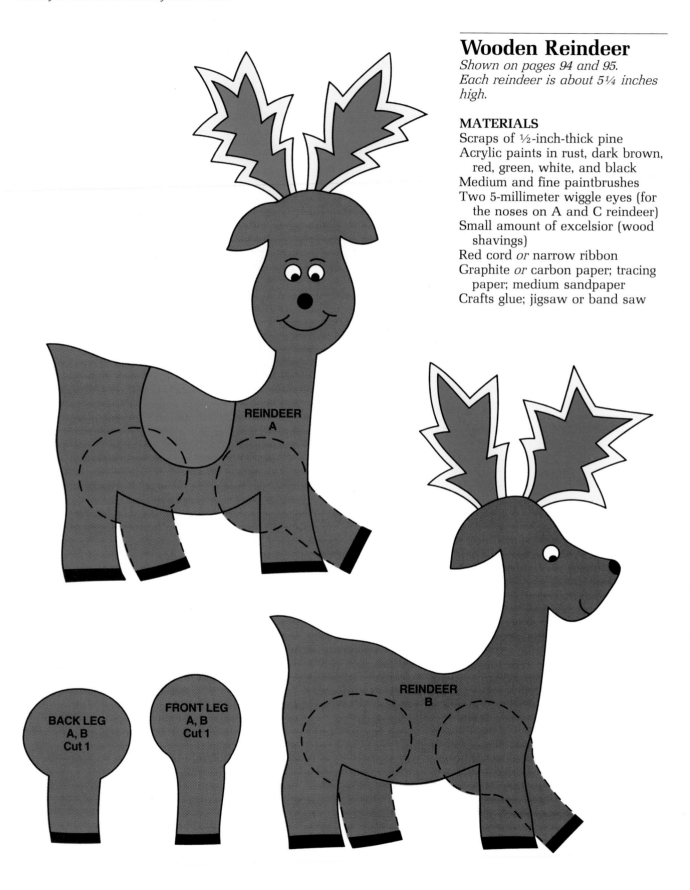

Wooden Reindeer

Shown on pages 94 and 95.
Each reindeer is about 5¼ inches high.

MATERIALS
Scraps of ½-inch-thick pine
Acrylic paints in rust, dark brown, red, green, white, and black
Medium and fine paintbrushes
Two 5-millimeter wiggle eyes (for the noses on A and C reindeer)
Small amount of excelsior (wood shavings)
Red cord *or* narrow ribbon
Graphite *or* carbon paper; tracing paper; medium sandpaper
Crafts glue; jigsaw or band saw

REINDEER A

REINDEER B

BACK LEG A, B Cut 1

FRONT LEG A, B Cut 1

INSTRUCTIONS

Trace full-size patterns, *opposite* and *below,* onto tracing paper. Then transfer separate outlines for body and leg patterns for each deer onto pine using graphite paper.

Using a jigsaw, cut out bodies. (Antlers and bodies are cut as one piece.) Cut separate legs for each reindeer as indicated on patterns. Sand edges.

To paint the reindeer, thin the rust paint with water until it is the con-sistency of a liquid stain. Paint the bodies and legs of the reindeer, leaving the antlers unpainted. Let all pieces dry completely.

Transfer the design details from the patterns to the reindeer. With dark brown paint, paint the hooves, noses, and mouths. To make noses for reindeer A and C, paint wiggle eyes brown and glue in place.

Using a fine brush, paint a dark brown line on the antlers about ⅛ inch from the edge. When dry, paint the area inside the brown line with green paint that has been thinned with water.

Paint the eyes white. When dry, paint a black dot inside each eye. Paint eyebrows brown. On reindeer A, paint the blanket on its back green and the heart red. (See photo on page 95.) Add white dots around the heart and green dots to blanket's edge. Paint a red heart on the chest of reindeer C.

When all pieces are painted and dry, glue legs in place, checking to see that each reindeer stands or sits properly before allowing the glue to dry completely.

After legs have dried, glue bits of wood-shaving hair at the bases of the antlers. To finish, tie a red cord or ribbon bow around each reindeer's neck.

REINDEER
C

LEG
C, D
Cut 4

REINDEER
D

Season of the Heart

Here are hearts to stitch and hearts to paint, a few to whittle and one to cut and paste—in short, a whole treasury of trims and trinkets for you to craft, all inspired by this much-loved symbol of the season.

Stitch the small Noel sampler, *left,* in homage to the holiday—perhaps as a gift for yourself or a special friend. Captured here in cross-stitch are a few of our favorite things: lots of hearts to be sure, but bunnies and kittens as well, plus a small cottage, a pretty quilt block, and a well-shaped Christmas tree just waiting to be trimmed.

As trims for your own tree, or to stockpile as gifts, cross-stitch a batch of these winsome lace-edged ornaments, *right,* in muted country colors. Work with single strands of wool tapestry yarn, using light and dark shades of the same color. Then, back each heart with felt and trim with a flourish of purchased lace. Ornaments measure about 4½ by 5 inches, excluding trim.

Here are two trees stunningly trimmed with a mixture of wood and needlework ornaments.

Delicate shadow-quilted hearts in soft pastel shades, *left,* are artfully combined with cutout wooden hearts painted in soft complementary colors. The quilted hearts are delicately stitched and lightly stuffed. The wooden hearts are trimmed with satin bows and purchased ribbon roses—a charming blend of hard and soft craft techniques.

The smaller tree, *below,* displays plump, wooden hearts made of pine. These were cut from ½-inch lumber with a jigsaw, filed and sanded to soften the edges, and finally stained and waxed to create their satiny finishes.

Completing this lighthearted country look are tiny bundles of ornamental wheat and simple squares of hardanger embroidery worked on natural color linen, both trimmed with red bows and hanging loops of gold thread.

Pretty painted finishes, in combed and sponged patterns, turn purchased wooden hearts into charming country-style ornaments, *below*.

First, a base coat of red or green acrylic paint is brushed on both sides of the heart and allowed to dry. For the combed finish, a coat of white acrylic is brushed on and furrowed with a cardboard comb while the paint is still wet.

For the sponge-painted design, lightly dab a scrap of sponge in white paint and then quickly pat it over the base coat. Accents of gold or silver metallic paint can be added to either finish, if you like.

At *right*, a cut-paper tribute to a timeless family scene: Mother and baby read by the fire, while father and children build a snowman below. Framed by these two vignettes is a candle-laden tree centered in a heart. An entire tale is told in silhouette by this piece done in scherenschnitte (or cut paper) and the framed result is enchanting.

An imaginative mix of small ornaments trim these two trees.

Dainty heart-shaped baskets of tooled copper foil, *below,* are nicely paired with rustic hearts of painted wood for a plain-and-fancy version of a country-theme tree.

Each copper basket is filled with baby's-breath and trimmed with narrow slivers of red satin ribbon. In contrast, the painted hearts hang from rough-and-tumble bows of homey jute twine. Both the wood and copper ornaments

measure less than 1½ inches across.

The cross-stitch stockings, *right,* are only slightly larger: 2½ inches from top to toe. The six simple patterns are worked in two strands of floss on 14-count even-weave fabric. Names and

outline figures are added in backstitch.

Personalized with a name or greeting, these plump little stockings make sweet gifts for friends and neighbors—and also can double as clever gift tags for special presents.

Noel Sampler

Shown on page 98.
Finished size is 9½x9½ inches.
Design is 107x107 stitches.

MATERIALS

20x20-inch piece of white
    hardanger
DMC embroidery floss: 2 skeins
    each of dark Christmas red (498)
    and dark forest green (987); 1
    skein *each* of Christmas red
    (321), dark topaz (781),
    Christmas gold (783), medium
    copper (920), light copper (922),
    dark antique blue (930), medium
    antique blue (931), forest green
    (989), mauve (3687), and medium
    mauve (3688)

INSTRUCTIONS

The pattern and color key for the
sampler are on page 107. If you like,
you can bind the edges of the hardanger with masking tape or turn
under a small hem.

Measure 5 inches down from the
top and 5 inches in from the left side
of the hardanger; begin stitching the
upper left-hand corner of the border
here. Use three plies of floss and
work the cross-stitches over two
threads of fabric. Complete cross-
stitch before adding details.

Outline the cats and rabbits with
dark Christmas red (498) backstitch,
using one ply of floss. Using Christmas red (321), add three French
knots to each cat's wreath; add two
French knots to each of the rabbits'
wreaths.

When all stitching is complete,
steam-press the stitchery on the
wrong side.

Frame the sampler as desired.

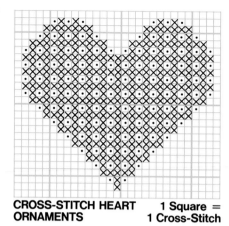

CROSS-STITCH HEART   **1 Square =**
ORNAMENTS   **1 Cross-Stitch**

Cross-Stitch Heart Ornaments

Shown on pages 98 and 99.
Finished heart is 5x4½ inches,
including lace.

MATERIALS
For 12 ornaments

36x12-inch piece of white 6-count
    Herta cloth
Paternayan 3-ply Persian yarn: 9
    strands *each* of dark violet (322),
    light violet (324), dark blue (511),
    light blue (513), dark green (610),
    light green (612), light gold (702),
    dark gold (700), dark copper
    (880), light copper (883), dark red
    (968), and light red (971)
36x12-inch piece of white felt
36x12-inch piece polyester fleece
36x24-inch piece fusible webbing
6 yards narrow flat lace
3 yards ¼-inch-wide white ribbon
Masking tape
Sewing thread

INSTRUCTIONS

Bind edges of Herta cloth with
masking tape. With sewing thread,
baste the outlines of twelve 6x6-
inch squares on fabric.

The pattern, *above,* does not re-
quire a color key. To stitch the
hearts, divide the yarn into color
groups, such as light green with dark
green and light red with dark red.
For one green heart, use light green
for the Xs and dark green for the
dots; for the other green heart, reverse colors and use light green for
the dots and dark green for the Xs.
Repeat for remaining color groups.

Center and stitch the hearts within each basted square. Use two plies
of yarn and work the cross-stitches
over one thread of fabric.

When stitching is finished, steam-
press on the wrong side. Cut along
basting lines to separate ornaments.

Cut fleece, felt, and fusible webbing into 6-inch squares. Following
the manufacturer's instructions, fuse
webbing to back of each heart and
to one side of the felt squares.

To assemble an ornament, layer
the felt (fusible side up), the fleece,
and the stitchery (right side up).
Topstitch around the heart outline
through all layers just inside the
edges of the outer stitches. Trim
away excess fabric, fleece, and felt
⅛ inch beyond stitching line.

Cut the ribbon into 9-inch lengths;
fold each into a loop. Tack the ends
to the back of the heart at top center.
Topstitch lace to stitched outline,
easing and clipping as necessary to
form rounded edges and points.

Shadow-Quilted Heart Ornaments

Shown on page 100.
Finished ornaments are about
4 inches wide.

MATERIALS

Scraps of dark red, blue, gold,
    green, and ivory cotton fabrics
¼ yard of ivory polyester organza
Sewing thread to match fabrics
Red, blue, green, and gold colored
    pencils or markers
No. 10 quilting needle
Plastic-coated freezer paper
Water-soluble marker
Glue stick
Polyester fiberfill
Gold metallic thread

INSTRUCTIONS

Preshrink and press all fabrics.

Referring to the full-size patterns
on pages 108–110, lay freezer paper
(shiny side down) atop patterns.
Trace each design; add a ¾-inch
border to each freezer-paper pattern
(includes ¼-inch seam allowance).

continued

NOEL SAMPLER

1 Square = 1 Cross-Stitch

COLOR KEY

⊟ Red (321)
⊞ Dark Red (498)
⧄ Forest Green (989)
⬤ Dark Forest Green (987)
◯ Medium Antique Blue (931)
▲ Dark Antique Blue (930)
◪ Gold (783)

⊡ Topaz (781)
⊡ Medium Mauve (3688)
⊠ Dark Mauve (3687)
◼ Light Copper (922)
⊡ Medium Copper (920)
– Dark Red Backstitches (498)
s Red French Knots (321)

SHADOW-QUILTED ORNAMENTS

Full-Size Patterns

Lay ivory cotton background fabric over patterns. Trace all design lines onto fabric with a water-soluble marker.

Note the fabric color designation given on each pattern piece (R indicates red, Gr indicates green, B indicates blue, and G indicates gold). You can vary the color combinations, if desired.

To cut the colored fabric pieces for the design, begin with the most prominent color. Place the paper pattern atop the fabric of that color; affix with a warm iron. Taking care to cut along the lines between the pattern pieces and not into adjacent shapes, cut out each of the required pieces of that fabric color for each design. (*Note:* Adjacent petals or leaves of the same color may be cut as one piece.)

Using the glue stick, dab glue onto the background fabric, inside the outlines of the shapes just cut. Position the shapes on the background and carefully peel away the paper.

Position the freezer paper on the next color of fabric and repeat the process. Continue until all fabrics are affixed to the background. Clip all loose and frayed threads. Pieces should fit together well.

Lay a piece of organza over the prepared design. To secure organza, baste around edges or dab the glue stick in each corner.

Hand-quilt along all lines of the design, including blue lines. (Do not quilt the outside border line.) Use thread colors to match each design shape, or quilt the whole design in the thread color that matches the border fabric.

Cut away the ¾-inch border outline from each paper pattern to make a pattern for the border.

Lay the border pattern (shiny side down) onto a 6-inch square of colored fabric—this is for a heart- or crown-shaped frame around the appliquéd motif on the ivory background. Affix paper pattern to the fabric by pressing lightly with a warm iron. Trace around both sides of the outline with a water-soluble marker; then gently pull away the freezer paper. Cut out border.

Lay the border (right side up) over the design, matching outside edges. Secure border with basting stitches.

Using the point of a needle, turn the *inside* seam allowance under along the border line marked on the ivory; appliqué in place with tiny, hidden stitches. Remove all traces of marker.

Cut the back of the ornament from the same fabric as the border. Use the outer edge of the border pattern to trace the ornament shape onto the fabric.

With right sides together, sew front to back using ¼-inch seams. Leave a small opening in one side for turning. Trim, clip curves, turn, and press ornament.

Stuff ornament with fiberfill and slip-stitch opening closed. If you prefer, you can leave the ornament unstuffed and hand-quilt along the border stitching line.

Add a loop of gold thread to top of the ornament for hanging.

Wooden
Heart Cutouts

Shown on page 100.
Finished ornaments are about
4 inches wide.

MATERIALS
Scraps of ½-inch softwood
Jigsaw *or* band saw
Sandpaper
Acrylic paints; paintbrush
Gloss spray varnish
Ivory ribbon roses *or* other trim
⅜-inch-wide ivory satin ribbon
Gold metallic thread

INSTRUCTIONS
    Draw a 4-inch-wide heart on paper. Measure ⅝ inch from all sides to draw a smaller heart inside the first. Cut on both drawn lines.
    Using the border as a pattern, trace the shape onto wood scraps and cut out with the saw. Sand all surfaces smooth.
    Paint cutouts with two coats of acrylic; sand lightly between coats. Seal with two coats of varnish.
    Glue a loop of gold thread to top of the ornament for hanging. Trim the top of the heart with ribbon roses and a satin ribbon bow.

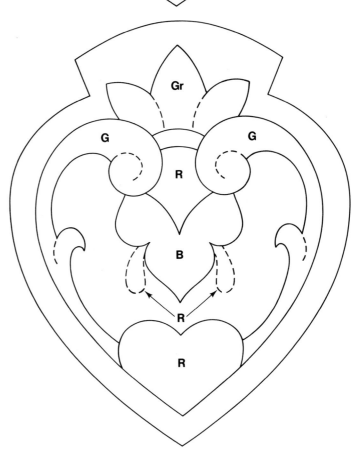

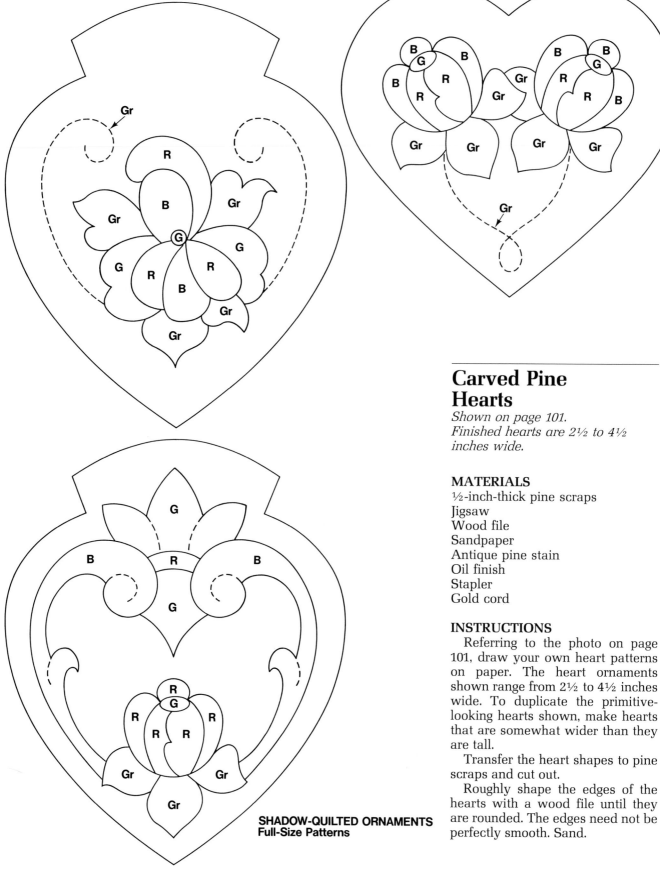

SHADOW-QUILTED ORNAMENTS
Full-Size Patterns

Carved Pine Hearts

Shown on page 101.
Finished hearts are 2½ to 4½
inches wide.

MATERIALS
½-inch-thick pine scraps
Jigsaw
Wood file
Sandpaper
Antique pine stain
Oil finish
Stapler
Gold cord

INSTRUCTIONS
Referring to the photo on page 101, draw your own heart patterns on paper. The heart ornaments shown range from 2½ to 4½ inches wide. To duplicate the primitive-looking hearts shown, make hearts that are somewhat wider than they are tall.

Transfer the heart shapes to pine scraps and cut out.

Roughly shape the edges of the hearts with a wood file until they are rounded. The edges need not be perfectly smooth. Sand.

Following manufacturer's directions, apply two coats of stain. Seal with oil finish. Staple gold cord to the back of the heart for hanging.

Wheat Bundle Ornaments

Shown on page 101.
Ornaments are about
5 inches high.

MATERIALS
Preserved decorative wheat
Florist's wire
½-inch-wide red grosgrain ribbon
Red or gold thread

INSTRUCTIONS
Gather five stalks of wheat; arrange them loosely so the heads do not all align.

Wrap bundle tightly with wire. Trim away straw so the bundle is about 5 inches high.

Tie a thread hanging loop around the wire. Tie a red ribbon bow around the wire; trim ribbon ends.

Hardanger Ornaments

Shown on page 101.
Finished ornaments are 4x4 inches.

MATERIALS
For four ornaments
12x12-inch piece of ivory
   hardanger
Sizes 5 and 8 ivory pearl cotton
Sizes 22 and 24 tapestry needles
Small embroidery scissors
⅛-inch-wide red satin ribbon
Gold metallic thread

INSTRUCTIONS
Cut hardanger into four 6-inch squares. Mark the center of each.

Refer to the specific instructions that follow for each of the four designs. (*Note:* The lines on each of the six figures, *above* and on page 112, represent one thread of fabric.)

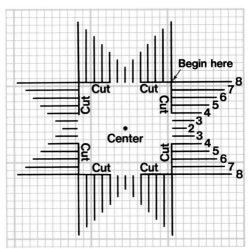

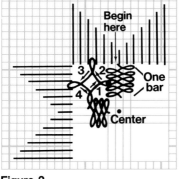

Figure 2

HARDANGER ORNAMENTS   **Figure 1**

The finishing instructions, which follow instructions for Design 4, are the same for all designs.

DESIGN ONE: Thread the larger needle with Size 5 pearl cotton. From the center, count six threads to the right and six threads up; bring the needle to the front of the fabric here. See Figure 1, *above*.

Make satin stitches as indicated in Figure 1; the numerals at the end of the right-hand stitches indicate the number of threads each stitch covers. Anchor the thread by running it under the satin stitches on the wrong side; trim thread.

To cut the fabric, refer to Figure 1. With the small scissors and beginning in any corner, cut four threads along each side of each corner, as indicated. Gently pull away loose threads as soon as both ends are cut. There should be four horizontal threads and four vertical threads remaining inside the star shape.

To work the needle weaving on the remaining threads, thread the smaller needle with Size 8 pearl cotton. Anchor the end of the thread by running it under the satin stitches on the wrong side. Bring the needle up adjacent to the satin stitches and in the middle of one set of four threads. Begin wrapping the four threads in a figure-eight fashion (see Figure 2). Wrap one whole bar, then turn the

corner and begin wrapping the second bar, stopping at the midpoint of the second bar.

At this point, work the filling stitch (see Figure 2) in the open square. When filling stitch is done, continue wrapping the second bar.

Wrap the two remaining bars and add the filling stitches.

DESIGN TWO: Use the larger needle and Size 5 pearl cotton. Refer to the instructions for Design One to find starting point of satin stitches. Refer to Figure 3 on page 112 and work satin stitches over the number of threads indicated. Cut the fabric threads as indicated.

Fill in the design center with wrapped bars and filling stitches as for Design One.

DESIGN THREE: Thread the larger needle with Size 5 pearl cotton. From center of fabric, count two threads to the right and two threads up. Begin stitching here. Referring to Figure 4 on page 112, work satin stitches; complete the 13 stitches of the first point. Slide the needle under satin stitches on the wrong side of the fabric to return to the center and begin the second point. Repeat until all eight points are stitched.

continued

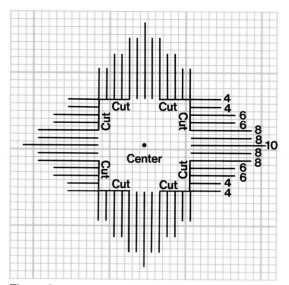

Figure 3

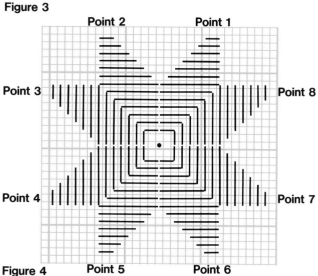

Point 2   Point 1

Point 3   Point 8

Point 4   Point 7

Figure 4   Point 5   Point 6

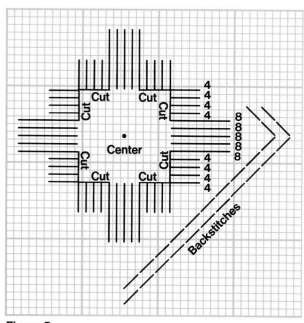

Center

Backstitches

Figure 5

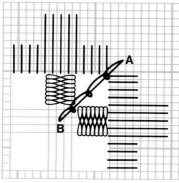

A

B

Figure 6

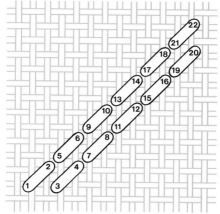

Figure 7

DESIGN FOUR: Using the larger needle and Size 5 pearl cotton, refer to the instructions for Design One to find starting point of satin stitches. Refer to Figure 5, *left,* and work satin stitches over the number of threads shown. Cut fabric threads as indicated.

Referring to the instructions for Design One, work needle weaving along all four bars, omitting the filling stitches.

To make the diagonal stitch in each open square, refer to Figure 6. Thread the smaller needle with Size 8 pearl cotton and bring it up at point A on the diagram and down at point B. Working back toward the outer corner, wrap the thread three times around itself, and insert the needle back through the fabric at point A. (*Note:* When wrapping the diagonal thread, keep the wrapping thread snug, but not so tight that it puckers the fabric.) Slide the needle under the satin stitches on the wrong side of the fabric and bring it up again at a point that corresponds with point A in the next adjacent corner. Repeat until all four diagonal stitches are completed.

To outline the design, use Size 8 pearl cotton and the smaller needle. Count eight threads from the middle stitch of the long satin stitches on any side. Referring to Figure 7, work a row of backstitch around the design. Continue in this manner until you reach the center of the next group of long satin stitches. Then turn the corner and repeat until you form a square around the center motif. Work a second outline square two threads inside the first square.

FINISHING: Count 25 threads from the center of stitchery to the top; cut and pull out this thread. Repeat on the three remaining sides. Count three more threads past the vacant thread; cut and pull out this thread on all four sides.

Work small buttonhole stitches between pulled threads around all four sides. The purled edge should be toward the outside of the square.

Trim threads evenly beyond the buttonhole stitches; remove cross threads to create fringe. Trim fringe so ornament is 4 inches square.

Tack a ribbon bow in one corner of each ornament and hang from a gold thread loop.

Comb- and Sponge-Painted Ornaments
Shown on page 102.

MATERIALS
Purchased wooden heart cutouts
Red, green, and ivory acrylic
   paints
Fine sandpaper
Gold and silver metallic paints
   (optional)
Paintbrushes; sponge
Medium-weight cardboard
Red and green ribbon
Matte-finish acrylic spray

INSTRUCTIONS
Sand cutouts lightly.

Paint both sides of hearts with two coats of red or green acrylic. Sand lightly between coats. Make an equal number of red and green hearts.

For comb-painting, make sure one edge of the cardboard is straight. Cut small notches in the straight edge. Paint one side of a heart with ivory paint. Working quickly while paint is still wet, drag notched cardboard through paint to form zigzag lines. Let dry.

For sponge-painting, cut a small piece of sponge, and pour a small amount of ivory paint onto a paper plate or piece of aluminum foil. Dip the sponge into the paint, and tap away the excess onto a paper towel. Working quickly with a light touch, dab the ivory paint onto the heart. Let dry. To add gold or silver accents, cut another piece of sponge and repeat with metallic paints.

Seal the ornaments with acrylic spray and hang from ribbon loops.

Heart-Shaped Scherenschnitte
Shown on page 103.
Finished design is 6¾x8¾ inches.

MATERIALS
9x12-inch piece of black
   scherenschnitte paper
Manicure scissors or crafts knife
Tracing paper; graphite paper

INSTRUCTIONS
Using the graphite paper, transfer the pattern on page 114 onto tracing paper. With a No. 2 pencil, color the back side of the tracing.

Fold black paper in half lengthwise so the white side is facing out. Match the folded edge of the tracing (colored side down) with the folded edge of the scherenschnitte paper. Draw over the lines to transfer the design to the scherenschnitte paper. Unfold the paper and trace the year of the cutting.

For greater success, begin cutting the areas along the folded line first.

Unfold the design to cut away the date. Then proceed to cut out the outer areas.

Lightly press the design with a warm iron on the back side of the cutting. Frame as desired.

Wooden Heart Ornaments
Shown on page 104.
Finished hearts are 1½ inches wide.

MATERIALS
Scraps of ½-inch softwood
Jigsaw; drill and bit
Sandpaper
Red acrylic paints
Paintbrushes
Glue
Matte-finish acrylic spray
Masking tape
Heavy jute twine

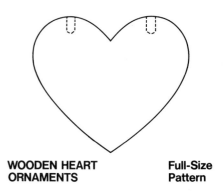

WOODEN HEART ORNAMENTS   **Full-Size Pattern**

INSTRUCTIONS
Referring to pattern, *above,* transfer heart shape to wood and cut out. Sand edges and surfaces.

Cut two 8-inch lengths of twine. Wrap one end of each length tightly with masking tape. Using a drill bit that is about the same size as the wrapped end of twine, drill two holes into top of heart.

Paint the heart with two coats of red paint, sanding lightly between coats. Seal with acrylic spray.

Glue taped ends of twine in holes. Tie loose ends into bow, leaving about a 2½-inch loop. Trim ends of twine.

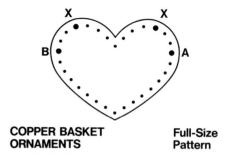

**COPPER BASKET
ORNAMENTS**

**Full-Size
Pattern**

Copper Basket Ornaments

Shown on page 104.
Baskets are 1⅜ inches wide.

MATERIALS
Copper tooling foil
Monofilament
⅛-inch-wide red *or* green satin
 ribbon (24 inches for each
 ornament)
Dried baby's-breath *or* other
 preserved or artificial foliage
Hammer and small nail
Tracing paper

INSTRUCTIONS
Trace pattern, *above,* and use the cutout shape to mark the outline of the heart on the copper foil. Cut two hearts for each basket. Layer the hearts and use the hammer and nail to punch about 30 evenly spaced holes around the outside edge of both layers at the same time.

Using monofilament, whipstitch the lower parts of the hearts together. Begin stitching at A and end at B. Secure monofilament with knots.

Bend the tops of the hearts apart slightly to form a basket.

Cut three 8-inch lengths of ribbon. For front handle, run the ends of one length through holes indicated by Xs on the pattern. Knot ribbon inside and trim ends. Repeat for back handle, making sure handles are even. Tie handles together with a bow, using the third length of ribbon. Trim baby's-breath to about 1¾ inches. Fill basket.

HEART-SHAPED SCHERENSCHNITTE   **Full-Size Pattern**

Cross-Stitch Sock Ornaments

Shown on page 105.
Ornaments are 2¼ inches high.

MATERIALS

Small amounts of tan 14-count
  even-weave fabric
1 skein each of DMC embroidery
  floss listed in color key, *below*
Scraps of red pindot fabric
Polyester fiberfill

INSTRUCTIONS

Referring to patterns, *right*, cross-stitch sock fronts using two strands of floss and working each stitch over one thread of fabric.

All backstitches are indicated by straight lines on the patterns. Add names or other greetings to the tops of the three border designs, using a backstitch alphabet of your choice.

Add grid pattern to holly motif sock with red backstitches.

For the reindeer sock, work the outline of the reindeer with medium gray backstitches; add a medium gray French knot for its eye and red French knots to the wreath around its neck.

For patchwork sock, add medium green backstitches to the heel; work all other backstitches with red.

For the striped stocking, work the center stripe of each three-stripe group in green; work outer stripes of each group in red.

Place stitcheries atop red fabric with right sides facing. Stitch together, following the outlines of the socks as a guide; leave top edges open. Trim excess fabric to ⅛-inch seam allowance; clip curves, turn, and press. Stuff with fiberfill and slip-stitch top opening closed. Add a floss loop for hanging.

COLOR KEY
⊞ Red (321)
▣ Medium Green (700)
⊟ Light Green (703)
◨ Gray (318)
☑ White
• French Knot
— Backstitches

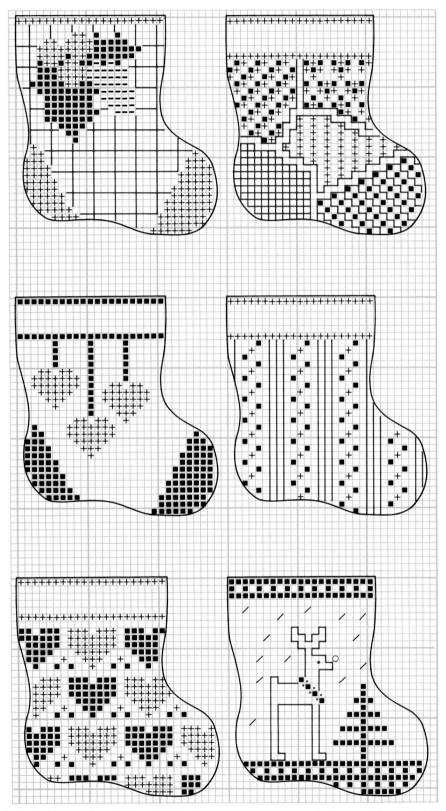

CROSS-STITCH SOCK ORNAMENTS

1 Square = Cross-Stitch

Knit and Crochet with Red and Green

If one of these crafts is your forte, then use your talents to crochet a festive granny-style afghan or to knit an oversized stocking—great holiday accents to use up lots of scrap yarns in your workbasket.

The 48x64-inch granny afghan, *left,* works up into four beds of red Christmas posies bordered by green paths. The three-dimensional flowers are easy to crochet, and the light and dark shades of red and green add color and pattern interest.

Experienced stocking knitters will enjoy the challenge of the two knitted stockings, *right.* The striped stocking uses different stitch patterns for each red stripe and has a leafy cuff trimmed with berries. The checkered stocking features a knitted-in design and a lacy cuff.

Instructions for all three projects begin on page 118.

Granny-Square Afghan

Shown on pages 116 and 117. Finished size is about 64x48 inches.

MATERIALS

Aarlan Cristal (50-gram ball): 5 balls of No. 4641 white (A); 4 balls of No. 4631 red (B); 3 balls of No. 4642 maroon (C); 12 balls of No. 4644 forest green (D); and 11 balls of No. 4632 Christmas green (E)

Size G aluminum crochet hook, *or* size to obtain gauge given below

Yarn needle

Abbreviations: See page 84.
Gauge: Finished squares measure 4x4 inches.

INSTRUCTIONS

GREEN SQUARES: Make 34 squares with color E and 36 squares with color D. Ch 8; join with sl st to form ring.

Rnd 1: Ch 3, in ring work 3 dc, ch 1; (4 dc, ch 1) 3 times; join with sl st to top of beg ch-3; sl st in each of next 3 dc and into first ch-1 sp.

Rnd 2: **Ch 3, in ch-1 sp work 2 dc, ch 1, 3 dc—beg corner shell made;** ch 1, dc bet second and third dc of next 4-dc shell, ch 1, * **in corner ch-1 sp work 3 dc, ch 1, 3 dc—corner shell made;** ch 1, dc bet second and third dc of next 4-dc shell, ch 1; rep from * twice more; join with sl st to top of beg ch-3; sl st in each of next 2 dc and into corner ch-1 sp.

Rnd 3: Work beg corner shell, ch 1, (2 dc in next ch-1 sp, ch 1) twice; * work corner shell in ch-1 sp of corner; ch 1, (2 dc in next ch-1 sp, ch 1) twice; rep from * twice more; join with sl st to top of beg ch-3; sl st to corner sp.

Rnd 4: Work beg corner shell, ch 1, (2 dc in next ch-1 sp, ch 1) 3 times; work corner shell in ch-1 sp of corner; ch 1, (2 dc in next ch-1 sp, ch 1) 3 times; rep from * twice more; join with sl st to top of beg ch-3; fasten off.

D	E	D	E	D	E	D	E	D	E	D
E	1	1	1	1	D	2	2	2	2	E
D	1	2	2	1	E	2	1	1	2	D
E	1	2	2	1	D	2	1	1	2	E
D	1	2	2	1	E	2	1	1	2	D
E	1	2	2	1	D	2	1	1	2	E
D	1	1	1	1	E	2	2	2	2	D
E	D	E	D	E	D	E	D	E	D	E
D	2	2	2	2	E	1	1	1	1	D
E	2	1	1	2	D	1	2	2	1	E
D	2	1	1	2	E	1	2	2	1	D
E	2	1	1	2	D	1	2	2	1	E
D	2	1	1	2	E	1	2	2	1	D
E	2	2	2	2	D	1	1	1	1	E
D	E	D	E	D	E	D	E	D	E	D

GRANNY-SQUARE AFGHAN

POSY SQUARE: Make 48 of each color combination.

First color combination: With C, ch 8; join with sl st to form ring.

Rnd 1: Ch 1, * sc in in next ch, 5 hdc in next ch; rep from * twice, end sc in next ch, 5 hdc in sl st; join with sl st to beg ch-1; fasten off.

Rnd 2: Turn; with wrong side facing and working into *back lps* on each st for this rnd only, join D in first hdc of any 5-hdc group; * sc in each of next 5 hdc, establish corner by working sc in center ring, pulling st tightly; rep from * 3 times more; join with sl st to first sc of rnd; sl st in next 2 sc.

Rnd 3: Ch 4, sk 2 sc, * in corner sc work **3 dc, ch 1, 3 dc—corner shell made;** ch 1, sk 2 sc, dc in next sc, ch 1; rep from * twice more; work corner shell in corner sc; ch 1, join with sl st to third ch of beg ch-4; sl st to next ch-1 sp.

Rnd 4: Ch 3, dc in same ch-1 sp, ch 1, * work corner shell in ch-1 sp of corner shell; ch 1, (2 dc in next ch-1 sp, ch 1) twice; rep from * twice more; work corner shell in ch-1 sp of corner shell, ch 1, 2 dc in next ch-1 sp, ch 1; join with sl st to top of beg ch-3; fasten off.

Rnd 5: Join A in any ch-1 corner sp; ch 3, in same corner sp work 2 dc, ch 1, 3 dc; ch 1, (2 dc in next ch-1 sp, ch 1) 3 times; * work corner shell

in ch-1 sp of next corner shell; ch 1, (in next ch-1 sp work 2 dc, ch 1) 3 times; rep from * twice more; join with sl st to top of beg ch-3; fasten off.

Turn square so right side of Rnd 1 is facing. Join B to front lp of first hdc of any 5-hdc group of Rnd 1 and work sc in same st; working in *front lps*, work 2 hdc in next st, 3 dc in next st, 2 hdc in next st, sc in next st; * in next 5-hdc group work sc in first st, 2 hdc in next st, 3 dc in next st, 2 hdc in next st, sc in last st; rep from * twice more; fasten off.

Second color combination: Work as for first posy square, substituting B for C, C for B, and E for D. Use A as for first color combination.

ASSEMBLY: Lay out squares according to diagram, *left.* Place posy squares with first color combination at each square on the chart labeled with a numeral 1; place posy squares with second color combinations at each square on the chart labeled with a 2. Place a forest green square at each square on the chart labeled with a D and a Christmas green square for each square on the chart labeled with an E.

With the yarn needle, whipstitch squares together. Refer to tip on page 121 for additional information on sewing squares together.

BORDER: *Rnd 1:* With right side facing, join B in first st to left of any corner; * work sc in each st of each square to corner; do not work sc into seams bet squares. In corner work 2 sc, ch 2, 2 sc; rep from * around; join with sl st to first sc.

Rnd 2: Ch 2, work hdc in each sc around; in each corner ch-2 sp work 2 hdc, ch 2, 2 hdc; join with sl st to top of beg ch-2; fasten off.

Rnd 3: Join D in eighth hdc to right of ch-2 corner sp, ch 2 (counts as first hdc), hdc in next 4 sts; **yo twice, insert hook from front to back to front around post of next sc of Rnd 1, draw up lp, (yo, draw through 2 lps) 3 times—front post treble crochet (fptrc) made;** ** hdc in next 2 sts; in corner ch-2 sp work 2 hdc, ch 2, 2 hdc; hdc in next 2 sts, fptrc in next st 2 rows below, * hdc in next 5 sts, fptrc in next st 2 rows below; rep from * across adjusting spacing of sts to end in 3rd hdc to right of next ch-2 corner sp. Rep from ** 3 times, ending last side at beg of rnd; join with sl st to top of beg ch-2; fasten off.

Rnd 4: Join E to second st to right of first fptrc before any corner of Rnd 3; ch 2, work fptrc around next hdc of previous rnd, hdc in next fptrc; (fptrc in next hdc, hdc in next 3 sts; in ch-2 corner sp work 2 hdc, ch 2, 2 hdc; hdc in next 3 sts, fptrc in next hdc, hdc in next fptrc; * fptrc in next hdc, hdc in next 3 sts, fptrc in next hdc, hdc in next fptrc; rep from * across to within 4 sts of next corner). Rep bet ( )s twice more; fptrc in next hdc, hdc in next 3 hdc; in corner ch-2 sp work 2 hdc, ch 2, 2 hdc; ** hdc in next 3 sts, fptrc in next hdc, hdc in next fptrc, fptrc in next hdc; rep from ** across, ending fptrc in beg ch-2 of Rnd 3, work hdc in next 2 sts; join with sl st to top of beg ch-2; fasten off.

Rnd 5: Join D in any st; work 1 rnd of reverse sc (crochet from left to right); join to first sc; fasten off.

Striped Stocking

Shown on page 117.
Finished stocking is 23½ inches from top to toe.

MATERIALS
Coats and Clark Red Heart worsted-weight yarn (3½-ounce skeins): 1 skein *each* of green No. 682 (A) and red No. 901 (B)
Scrap of contrasting-color yarn
Size 6 double-pointed knitting needles (dpn), *or* size to obtain gauge given below
Size 6 circular needle (11½-inch length)
Tapestry needle

Abbreviations: See page 85.
Gauge: Over st st, 6 sts = 1 inch.

INSTRUCTIONS
TOP BORDER: With A, cast on 8 sts.

Row 1 (right side): K 5, yo, k 1, yo, k 2—10 sts.

Row 2: P 6, **k into front and back of next st—inc made;** k 3—11 sts.

Row 3: K 4, p 1, k 1, yo, k 1, yo, k 4—13 sts.

Row 4: P 8, inc, k 4—14 sts.

Row 5: K 4, p 2, k 3, yo, k 1, yo, k 4—16 sts.

Row 6: P 10, inc, k 5—17 sts.

Row 7: K 4, p 3, k 4, yo, k 1, yo, k 5—19 sts.

Row 8: P 12, inc, k 6—20 sts.

Row 9: K 4, p 4, sl 1, k 1, psso, k 7, k 2 tog, k 1—18 sts.

Row 10: P 10, inc, k 7—19 sts.

Row 11: K 4, p 5, sl 1, k 1, psso, k 5, k 2 tog, k 1—17 sts.

Row 12: P 8, inc, k 2, p 1, k 5—18 sts.

Row 13: K 4, p 1, k 1, p 4, sl 1, k 1, psso, k 3, k 2 tog, k 1—16 sts.

Row 14: P 6, inc, k 3, p 1, k 5—17 sts.

Row 15: K 4, p 1, k 1, p 5, sl 1, k 1, psso, k 1, k 2 tog, k 1—15 sts.

Row 16: P 4, inc, k 4, p 1, k 5—16 sts.

Row 17: K 4, p 1, k 1, p 6, sl 1, k 2 tog, psso, k 1—14 sts.

Row 18: P 2 tog, bind off next 5 sts as follows: k 1, pass st on right needle over k st; continue to bind off next 4 sts, k 1, p 1, k 5—8 sts.

Rep rows 1–18 three times more. Bind off rem 8 sts and sew bound-off edge to cast-on edge.

STOCKING: With B and circular needle, pick up and k 56 sts around garter st edge of border. Join, place marker for end of rnd; p 1 rnd.

Rnd 2: * K 4, p 4; rep from * around.

Rnd 3: * K 5, p 3; rep from * around.

Rnd 4: * K 6, p 2; rep from * around.

Rnd 5: * K 7, p 1; rep from * around.

Rnd 6: P all sts; break off B.

Rnds 7–19: With A, k all sts; break off A.

Rnd 20: With B, k all sts.

Rnd 21: Work in seed st as follows: * k 1, p 1; rep from * around.

Rnds 22–28: Keeping to seed st on each rnd, p the k sts and k the p sts. At end of Rnd 28, break off B.

Rnds 29–41: With A, k all sts; at end of Rnd 41, break off A.

Rnd 42: With B, k all sts.

Rnd 43: * K 3, p 1; rep from * around.

Rnd 44: * P 1, k 3; rep from * around.

Rnd 45: * K 1, p 1, k 2; rep from * around.

Rnd 46: * K 2, p 1, k 1; rep from * around.

Rnd 47: Rep Rnd 43.

Rnd 48: Rep Rnd 44.

Rnd 49: Rep Rnd 45; break off B.

Rnds 50–63: With A, k all sts; break off A.

Rnd 64: With B, k all sts.

Rnds 65–67: * P 1, k 3; rep from * around.

Rnd 68: P all sts.

Rnds 69–71: Rep Rnd 65; break off B.

Rnds 72–78: With A, k all sts, ending last rnd within 14 sts of end of the rnd marker.

PREPARE FOR HEEL: With contrasting color, k next 28 sts. Sl these 28 sts back to left needle and k again with A. *Note:* The contrast color will be removed later to make heel.

Rnds 79–84: With A, k all sts; break off A.

Rnd 85: With B, k all sts.

Rnds 86–87: * K 2, p 2; rep from * around.

Rnds 88–89: * P 2, k 2; rep from * around.

Rnds 90–91: Rep rnds 86–87.

Rnd 92: K all sts; break off B.

Rnds 93–105: With A, k all sts; break off A.

Rnd 106: With B, k all sts.

Rnd 107: * P 1, k 3; rep from * around.

Rnd 108: * P 2, k 2; rep from * around.

Rnd 109: * P 3, k 1; rep from * around.

Rnd 110: P all sts.

Rnd 111: Rep Rnd 109.

Rnd 112: Rep Rnd 108.

Rnd 113: Rep Rnd 107; break off B.

Rnds 114–126: With A, k all sts; break off A.

continued

TOE SHAPING: With B, k 1 rnd; change to dpn. *First needle:* K 11, k 2 tog, k 1; *second needle:* K 1, sl 1, k 1, psso, k 22, k 2 tog, k 1; *third needle:* K 1, sl 1, psso, k 11—52 sts.

Rnd 2: K all sts.

Rnd 3: First needle: K to within last 3 sts at end of first needle, k 2 tog, k 1; *second needle:* K 1, sl 1, k 1, psso, k to within 3 sts at end of second needle, k 2 tog, k 1; *third needle:* K 1, sl 1, k 1, psso, k to end of rnd—48 sts.

Rnd 4: K all sts.

Rep last 2 rnds until 20 sts rem, end after working Rnd 4; k 5, sl these 5 sts to third needle. Break off B, leaving a 15-inch yarn end. Weave toe sts tog using kitchener stitch.

HEEL SHAPING: Remove contrasting yarn, slipping lps to needles. (There will be 27 lps above the opening and 28 lps below.) Pick up 1 st at a corner—56 sts. Divide on dpn as for toe; finish as for toe with B.

FINISHING: Refer to tip box, *opposite,* for making cord and tassels. With A, make a 6-inch-long twisted cord. Make two tassels, one with A and one with B, that are about 3 inches long. Attach the tassels to each end of the cord. Loop center of cord through st at center back below top border. Center of cord will form hanging loop; tassels will prevent loop from pulling through.

With B, make clusters of three berries at lower edge of each leaf of top border using two side-by-side bullion stitches for each berry.

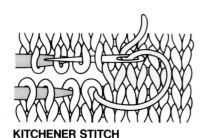

KITCHENER STITCH

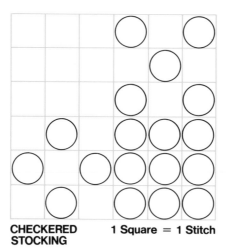

CHECKERED STOCKING   **1 Square = 1 Stitch**

Checkered Stocking

Shown on page 117.
Finished length of stocking is 23½ inches from top to toe.

MATERIALS

Coats and Clark Red Heart worsted-weight yarn (3½-ounce skeins): 1 skein *each* of green No. 682 (A) and red No. 901 (B)
Scrap of contrasting-color yarn
Size 6 double-pointed knitting needles (dpn), *or* size to obtain gauge given below
Size 6 circular needle (11½-inch length)
Tapestry needle
Yarn bobbins

Abbreviations: See page 85.
Gauge: Over st st, 6 sts = 1 inch.

INSTRUCTIONS

LACE BORDER PATTERN: *Rnd 1:* * P 1, yo, k 4, sl 1, k 2 tog, psso, k 4, yo; rep from * around.

Rnd 2: K all sts.
Rep these 2 rnds for pat.

STOCKING: *Note on two-color knitting:* When changing yarn colors, always twist new color around the color in use to avoid making holes. Carry unused color loosely across back, twisting it around the color in use every three or four stitches.

With A, cast on 60 sts; join, being careful not to twist. Place marker for end of rnd. K 1 rnd; p 1 rnd. Work Lace Border Pattern until length measures 4 inches, ending with Rnd 2. Change to st st; work even 1 rnd.

BEADING RND: * K 2 tog, yo; rep from * around. Work even 2 rnds.

Wind one bobbin with red yarn and one bobbin with green yarn.

Begin chart, *above left,* working even until total length measures 14 inches, ending last rnd 15 sts before end-of-rnd marker. Break off both A and B. K next 30 sts with contrasting yarn. Sl last 15 sts worked back to left needle; drop contrasting yarn. *Note:* Contrasting yarn will be removed later to work heel. Resume chart pat, working even until total length measures 20½ inches. Break off B.

TOE SHAPING: *Rnd 1:* With A, k 12, k 2 tog, k 1, place side marker, k 1, sl 1, k 1, psso, k 24, k 2 tog, k 1, place side marker, k 1, sl 1, k 1, psso, k 12.

Rnd 2: K all sts.

Rnd 3: (K to within 3 sts of side marker, k 2 tog, k 1, sl marker, k 1, sl 1, k 1, psso) twice; k to end of rnd.

Rnd 4: K all sts.

Rep last 2 rnds until 20 sts rem, changing to dpn as needed; k 5, break off yarn, leaving a long end.

Weave the top of the toe using kitchener stitch.

HEEL SHAPING: Remove the contrasting yarn, slipping lps to needles. (There will be 29 lps above the opening and 30 lps below.) Pick up 1 st at one corner—60 sts. Divide onto dpn and work as for toe with A.

FINISHING: Refer to information, *opposite,* to make twisted cord and pom-poms. With B, make a 34-inch-long twisted cord. Thread the cord through beading row. Make two pom-poms with equal amounts of red and green yarns. Fasten a pom-pom to each end of cord.

FINISHING TOUCHES FOR KNITTING AND CROCHETING

Following are helpful tips for completing the crocheted afghan and knitted stockings shown on pages 116 and 117.

ASSEMBLING GRANNY SQUARES: Many crocheters choose to join granny squares as they work; others prefer to complete all the individual units before assembling any of them. In either case, there are several ways to join squares and other motifs.

If you're joining squares after all are completed, lay them out in the proper placement on the floor. It's easiest to join all of the squares into long rows and then join together the rows.

To whipstitch squares, place two squares together with right sides facing. Using a yarn needle threaded with yarn that matches the squares, sew together corresponding stitches of each of the two squares. You can sew these squares together by working under both loops or the back loops of the squares. When you sew under the back loops, the square will have a running outline of the square on the right side.

To crochet squares together, use the same procedure for laying out the pieces. You can single crochet or slip-stitch pieces together. Crocheted seams are bulkier, have less elasticity than sewn seams, and are more noticeable on the wrong side. Knitted and crocheted pieces should never be joined with machine stitching.

TWISTED CORD: This cord, which is suitable for trimming many types of needlework projects, resembles purchased cable cord. For best results, make the cord from the same yarn used for the project.

Determine finished length of the cord, then cut four lengths of yarn, each three times the finished length. For example, for a 24-inch-long finished cord, cut four 72-inch lengths of yarn. Align the strands and knot them together at both ends, about 1 inch from the ends.

Insert a knitting needle or wooden skewer through each knot. With another person holding one needle and keeping the strands taut, twist the yarn between thumb and fingers until strands are tightly twisted and begin to form a coil. Turn one end counterclockwise to uncoil the strands slightly.

Keeping the strands taut, find the midpoint of the cord, fold the two ends together, remove the needles or skewers, and knot two ends together. Holding the new knot firmly, smooth the halves together to form even twists.

Untie the first knots and trim evenly to make a small tassel. Knot the other end, unravel the ends slightly, and trim to make a similar tassel.

CROCHETED CORD: You can also crochet a length of chain stitches to make a cord. Make a chain slightly longer than the desired finished length. Slip-stitch in each chain across.

TASSELS: You can alter the size of tassels by changing the size of the loops and varying the number of loops you make.

Cut a 5-inch-wide piece of cardboard that is approximately the finished height of the tassel. Wind yarn around the cardboard to make loops, keeping the yarn loops tightly bunched. The number of times you wind the yarn depends upon how thick you want the tassel.

Cut the end of the yarn even with the bottom of the cardboard, and then cut a length to serve as the hanging thread or loop. Thread this length of yarn under the yarn loops and tie it securely. Slip the loops off the cardboard and, keeping the hanging thread at the top, smooth the loops together, and clip them at a point directly opposite the hanging thread knot. Trim the ends evenly to the desired length.

You can leave the tassel as it is, or tie a second strand around the bundle of yarn lengths below the original knot. Trim the ends of this strand evenly with the rest of the tassel.

POM-POMS: To make these round, fluffy balls, wind yarn around cardboard as for making tassels, except shorten the height of the cardboard strip and wind the yarn around the cardboard many more times. Then slip the yarn off the cardboard and tie the bundle securely around the middle. Clip *both* ends of the loops and trim carefully to form a spherical shape.

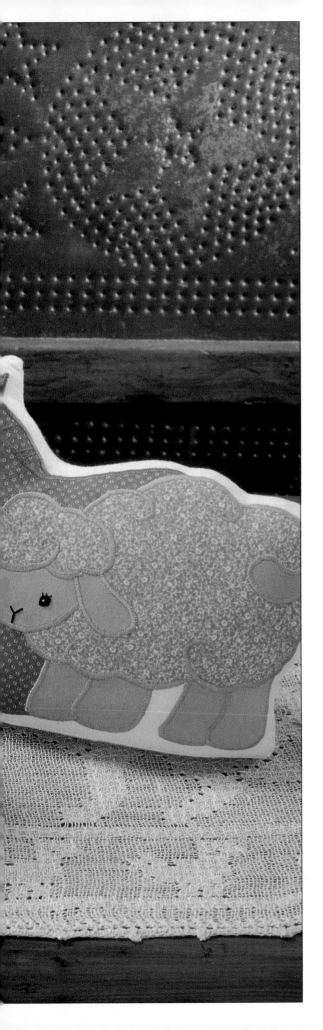

Celebrate the Christmas Story

Amid all the joys of gift-giving, merry gatherings, and moments shared with family and friends, we pause to recall the true meaning of this holiday season—the wondrous birth of the Christ Child.

This charming appliquéd crèche recalls the sweet simplicity of the long-ago scene in a manger in Bethlehem.

Figures of the Holy Family and a few friendly animals—a little donkey and a pair of lambs—are made of calico scraps and stitched to a muslin background. Note the artful mixture of large and small prints and the rows of narrow satin stitching used to outline the details on each figure.

Measuring from 6 to 10 inches tall, the soft-sculpture figures are weighted with dried beans, enabling them to stand straight and steady on any surface.

The crèche is displayed here on a lace table runner in front of the star-patterned, pierced-tin doors of an antique pie safe. But scattered straw, simple greenery or a manger built from twigs or wood scraps would make an equally effective setting.

Wherever and however it's displayed in your home, this simple crèche is a heart-warming reminder of the age-old Christmas story.

123

A galaxy of gold-flecked stars, *left,* cascades down a greenery-wrapped banister—a reminder of the single shining star that blazed in the heavens above Bethlehem on that wonderful night of nights.

The stars shining here are of white-painted tin speckled with gold. Cardboard may be substituted for the tin, if you prefer. Attach the stars to the garland of greens with loops of double-faced tape, as we did here, or use lengths of gold thread or ribbon looped through a hole drilled in one star point.

Full-size patterns for three sizes of stars can be found on page 134.

The six cross-stitch Chrismons, *right,* are so-called because each is inspired by one of the many symbols that early Christians associated with the life of Christ. The word "Chrismon" derives from "Christ" and "monogram."

These lovely designs are stitched on 14-count Aida cloth using light and dark gold floss and accents of gold metallic thread. Individually or as a set, they make particularly thoughtful gifts at Christmastime.

The Chrismons tradition began in 1957, when a Lutheran church group in Danville, Va., created some gold and white ornaments for their tree. Since then, many churches and families make a practice of decorating entire trees with Chrismons made in a variety of techniques.

Inspired by a beloved Christmas carol, this glorious cross-stitch sampler, *right,* is destined to become a treasured family heirloom. Hang it near the door to greet Christmas guests, or set it on an easel on the buffet sideboard as a holiday centerpiece.

Wherever it's hung or displayed, the sampler nearly sings with holiday spirit, extending its message of love, joy, and peace to one and all.

Combining a quartet of herald angels and a stylized Christmas border with more traditional sampler motifs of hearts and alphabets, this pattern also offers a feast of design elements to adapt for smaller projects.

Portions of the border motif, along with messages composed from the sampler alphabet,

make up the cards, *above.* Stitched with cotton floss on perforated paper that is then mounted on colored card stock, these mini-samplers make very special Christmas cards, each a tiny gift in itself, suitable for framing.

You also can make tree ornaments from the same patterns by stitching the designs on scraps of perforated paper and gluing them to red or green felt, cut to size. Add a bow at the center top and a loop of satin ribbon for hanging.

Make Christmas sachets by stitching the designs on scraps of even-weave fabric, backing the embroideries with calico, and stuffing the resulting pillows with potpourri. The sachets are perfect to keep on hand for last-minute gifts.

Soft-Sculpture Crèche

Shown on pages 122 and 123.
Finished figures range from 6 to 10 inches high.

MATERIALS

¾ yard of muslin
Small amounts of gray, tan, rose, blue, brown, dark green, and yellow print and floral stripe fabrics
Small amounts of gray, tan, brown, yellow, and light pink solid fabrics
Black, white, pink, red, rose, wine, and dark green embroidery floss
Dry cosmetic blush
Polyester fiberfill
Threads to match fabrics
Paper-backed fusible webbing
Cardboard; tissue paper
Air- or water-soluble marker
Dressmaker's carbon (optional)
Small plastic bags
Dried beans *or* sand
T-pins; carpet thread

INSTRUCTIONS

Refer to the full-size patterns on pages 130–133. Trace the outlines, facial features, and clothing details onto tissue to make master patterns. Trace the three separate base patterns as indicated for the different pieces.

Holding the pattern and muslin against a light source, trace entire pattern of each figure onto muslin with air-soluble marker. Or use the dressmaker's carbon to transfer the patterns to the muslin. Do not cut out the shapes until the appliquéing is complete.

Cut out a base for each figure from cardboard and muslin, adding ⅜-inch seam allowances to the muslin shapes.

For the appliqué patterns, place tissue paper atop the full-size patterns and trace each separate motif *or* one motif for adjoining sections (such as the lamb's face and ears). Add underlaps as needed. Label each tissue pattern, and cut out.

Fuse the webbing to the *wrong sides* of the appliqué fabrics *before cutting out the shapes.*

Pin tissue patterns atop the right sides of the appliqué fabrics and cut out. To reverse the pattern for the single lamb, pin tissue patterns atop *wrong sides* of the appliqué fabrics and cut out. Assemble the appliqué pieces and fuse in place on top of the muslin figures. Machine-zigzag-stitch around all of the appliquéd shapes with matching threads.

EMBROIDERY: Add facial details with the air-soluble marker; use dressmaker's carbon, if desired. Use two plies of floss for all embroidery unless otherwise noted.

Satin-stitch all eyes black; add eye accent with white French knot. Outline-stitch the noses pink (for the Infant) and rose (for Mary and Joseph); outline-stitch the smiles red (for the Infant) and wine (for Mary and Joseph). Use straight stitches and one ply of black for all eyelashes and animal noses. Color the cheeks *lightly* with blush.

ASSEMBLY: Cut out each shape, leaving ⅜-inch seam allowances around each figure. Cut out a matching back for each figure from muslin. Round all sharp angles into gradual curves.

Sew together the front and back of each figure with right sides facing; stitch along the seam lines and leave the bottom open. Trim and clip curves.

Machine-baste along the seam lines of the bottom and the base; clip. Sew bottom and fabric base together, matching points of the base with the side seams and leaving the center back open. Trim and turn figures to the right side.

Stuff top half of figure. Secure beans or sand inside plastic bag. Place bag and cardboard base inside figure. Poke additional fiberfill above bag and base until figure is firm. Close the opening securely with T-pins and stitch the opening closed with carpet thread. Tie matching floss into small bows and tack to headpieces.

Cross-Stitch Chrismons

Shown on page 125.
Ornaments are 3¾x3¾ inches.
Designs are 37x37 stitches.

MATERIALS
For six ornaments

12x36-inch piece of white 14-count Aida cloth
DMC embroidery floss: 2 skeins of dark gold (680) and 1 skein of light gold (676)
1½ yards of ¼-inch-wide gold metallic ribbon
Gold metallic thread
White sewing thread
Polyester fiberfill
Embroidery hoop
Tapestry needle

INSTRUCTIONS

Refer to the patterns, *opposite,* and transfer designs to graph paper for master patterns. Or stitch ornaments directly from the charts.

Baste outlines for six 6x6-inch squares on Aida cloth. Center and stitch a design within each outline. Use two plies of floss to work the cross-stitches and work each stitch over one thread of fabric.

Work all backstitches (indicated by red lines on the patterns) with dark gold (680), *except* work the three diagonal lines on the underbelly of each fish with light gold (676).

Steam-press the stitcheries on the wrong side.

Cut out ornaments along basting lines. Cut out six 6x6-inch backing squares from remaining Aida cloth. To assemble, place a stitchery and a backing square right sides together. Stitch around, three threads beyond outer border of ornament, and leaving an opening for turning. Trim fabric close to stitching and clip corners. Turn, stuff with fiberfill, and slip-stitch closed.

Cut gold metallic ribbon into 9-inch lengths. Tie into bows and tack to center top of each ornament; trim ribbon ends. Add a loop of gold metallic thread to hang.

Four Fish (Call of the Apostle Fishermen)

Crown and Cross (King of Kings)

Grapes (Holy Communion)

Wheat (Pentecost)

Burning Bush (God's Presence)

Olive Branch (Symbol of Hope)

CROSS-STITCH CHRISMONS

COLOR KEY
⊠ Dark Gold (680)
◎ Light Gold (676)

SOFT-SCULPTURE CRÈCHE: Full-Size Patterns

MARY

JOSEPH

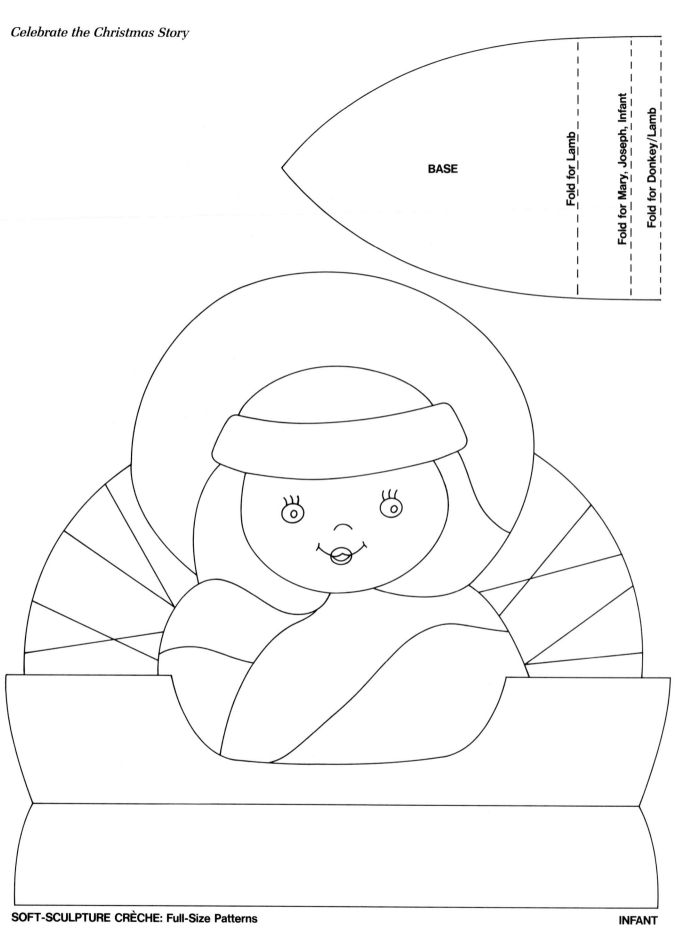

BASE

Fold for Lamb

Fold for Mary, Joseph, Infant

Fold for Donkey/Lamb

SOFT-SCULPTURE CRÈCHE: Full-Size Patterns

INFANT

DONKEY/LAMB

Painted Stars

Shown on page 124.
Stars are 3⅝ to 5½ inches wide.

MATERIALS

Scraps of sheet metal *or* medium-
   weight white cardboard
White paint; chalk pencil
Gold metallic paint
Stencil material; crafts knife
Paintbrushes
Sponges
Clear acrylic spray

INSTRUCTIONS

Transfer the three full-size star patterns on this page to metal with chalk pencil or to cardboard with a soft-lead pencil. Cut out the shapes; flatten the edges of the metal stars, if necessary.

Paint the metal stars with white paint. Touch up the edges of the cardboard shapes with white paint, if necessary.

The stars shown on page 124 are painted with gold in two different ways; one way has a gold star stenciled in the center of each star and the other has a sponge-painted trim along the edges of the stars.

To stencil the star shape, cut a stencil the size of the shaded areas on each of the full-size patterns. Dip sponge lightly in gold metallic paint; dab away excess on paper towels.

**PAINTED
STARS**

Full-Size Patterns

Center stencil on top of star and lightly fill in stencil area with gold, allowing some of the white background to show through.

For the stars with gold-trimmed edges, load the sponge with gold paint and dab around the edges of the star, painting about ¼ to ½ inch in from the edge.

Cross-Stitch Cards

Shown on page 126.

MATERIALS

14-count white perforated paper
DMC embroidery floss: Small amounts of deep pistachio green (319), medium pistachio green (320), and Christmas red (321)
Tapestry needle
Crafts glue
Graph paper; colored pencils (optional)
Red and green blank greeting cards and envelopes

INSTRUCTIONS

Use patterns, *above right,* or create your own designs, using the chart for the sampler shown on page 127 as a guide. (See pages 136 and 137 for the chart.) Use colored pencils and graph paper to chart your original designs before stitching, if desired.

Perforated paper is fragile and can tear or bend easily. Consider stapling it to a stretcher frame before you begin stitching. Stretcher frames are available in different sizes and can be purchased at needlecrafts supply stores.

Locate the center of the design on the chart and the center of the paper; begin stitching there. Use three plies of floss and work the cross-stitches over one square of the paper. Avoid pulling the floss too tightly when stitching.

When the stitching is complete, trim the paper at least one square beyond the cross-stitches. Glue the piece to the front of a blank greeting card. If desired, add ribbons or paper lace trims.

CROSS-STITCH CARDS

COLOR KEY
☐ **Medium Pistachio Green (320)**
▨ **Deep Pistachio Green (319)**
⊠ **Christmas Red (321)**

Christmas Angels Sampler

Shown on page 127.
Stitchery is about 14½x17½ inches.
Design is 179x219 stitches.

MATERIALS

25x36-inch piece of white 25-count Lugana cloth
DMC embroidery floss: 4 skeins *each* of deep pistachio green (319) and Christmas red (321); 3 skeins of medium pistachio green (320); 1 skein *each* of pale yellow (745), garnet (816), and flesh (948)
Gold metallic floss
Embroidery hoop; tapestry needle
Graph paper; colored pencils

INSTRUCTIONS

Referring to pattern on pages 136 and 137, transfer design onto graph paper or work from the chart.

On a separate piece of graph paper, and using the alphabet pattern on page 137, chart family names, initials, or other greeting. Center and transfer your names or greeting to the sampler chart under "Merry Christmas 1989," aligning the tops of the letters with line 1 and the bottoms of the letters with line 2. Or mark the vertical center of your chart and stitch directly from it onto the cloth.

Measure 5 inches down from the top and 5 inches in from the left side; begin stitching the upper left-hand corner of the border here. Use three plies of floss and work the cross-stitches over two threads of fabric. Depending on the weight of the gold metallic floss you are using, use as many plies of metallic floss as necessary to match the other embroidery floss.

Outline angels' sleeves with garnet (816) backstitches, using one ply of thread. Fill in the angels' wings with gold metallic backstitches.

Steam-press the stitchery on the wrong side and frame as desired.

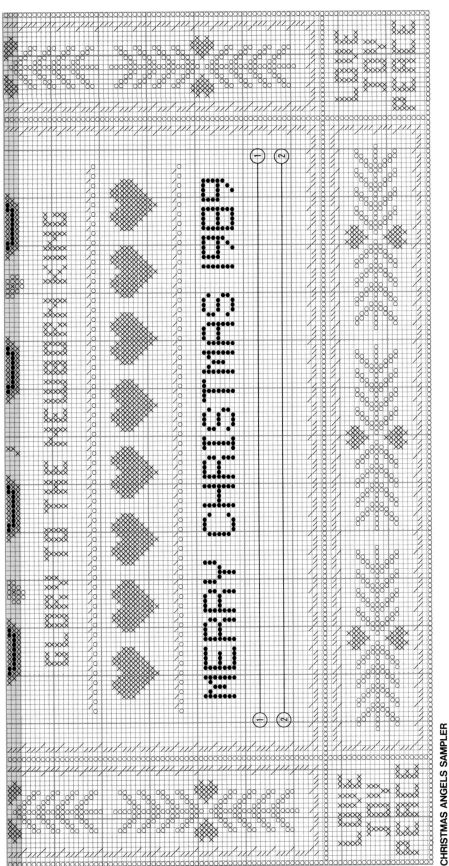

CHRISTMAS ANGELS SAMPLER

COLOR KEY
- ⊡ Medium Pistachio Green (320)
- ⊙ Deep Pistachio Green (319)
- ⊠ Christmas Red (321)
- ● Gold Metallic Floss
- ⊟ Flesh (948)
- ▣ Pale Yellow (745)

Made by Hand to Give with Love

One-of-a-kind gifts that showcase your special craft skills are welcome anytime of the year, but especially at Christmastime.

The handsome handmades in this chapter are sure to suit almost everyone on your holiday gift list.

At *right,* an elegant needlepoint monogram is a lovely way to personalize a pretty pillow for a special friend. On page 145, you'll find an entire alphabet of gorgeous Gothic initials.

For cross-stitch enthusiasts, there's the charming theme sampler.

It makes an ideal gift for friends or relatives who take pride in decorating their homes for the holidays.

Those whose specialty is working with natural materials can make the wooden jewelry. The pin, earrings, and necklace are formed from simple disks of wood that have been lovingly cured, sanded, and varnished to a soft, satiny sheen.

Any young lass would love to discover one of these ruffled beauties, *left,* beneath the tree on Christmas morning. To make a demure pinafore or the patchwork tabard, use a variety of prints and solids in traditional Christmas colors and trim the finished garments with ribbon and lace. Use scraps of the same materials to dress the muslin rag doll.

Full-size patterns for the pinafore's tulip appliqué and for the patchwork inset on the tabard are included in the projects' instructions. Scale patterns for both garments also are given (the pinafore in girls' sizes 6-8, the tabard in girls' sizes 4-6).

Both boys and girls, from tots to preteens, love animals. Make one or two of these playtime pets, *above right,* for a favorite youngster. The cat and dog jigsaw puzzles, each with six large pieces, are simple enough for toddlers to solve and sturdy enough to survive a nurseryful of kids. Cut the puzzles from 1¼-inch lumber with a table jigsaw and then use a woodburning tool to draw on the animals' faces.

The teetering fawn and floppy fox, *below right,* are made of washable acrylic fur and stuffed with squeezable fiberfill. The fawn sports a woolly winter scarf knit from yarn scraps. Use red and green as shown or knit it in a child's favorite school or team colors.

For a beautifully personalized Christmas stocking—one sure to be treasured for many Christmases to come—needlepoint or cross-stitch a monogram initial (patterns on page 145). Stitch it in red and cream, then piece the square into a patchwork stocking.

Assorted scraps of red and green fabrics, both prints and solids, were assembled to create the stocking, *right*. Note the sophisticated mixture of scale in the prints. To accent the design, couch strands of red tapestry yarn along the seam lines between each patch.

Alter the one basic pattern as many ways as you like to create the charming dolls. These diminutive darlings appeal to all ages, so when you pass them out to the little ones, don't be surprised if grown-ups want dolls of their own. Nestled among greenery and bearing miniature packages or tiny baskets of goodies, the dolls make adorable accents in a holiday setting.

With padded bottoms, the dolls will stand wherever you place them. Looped and braided skeins of brown, yellow, and russet pearl cotton are used to create their old-fashioned hairstyles. Their simple features are embroidered in cotton floss; use a spot of rouge to bring a maidenly blush to each fabric cheek.

For complete patterns and instructions, turn to page 155.

Monogrammed Pillow

Shown on pages 138 and 139.
Finished pillow is 17 inches
square, including ruffle.

MATERIALS

DMC Floralia 3-ply yarn: Two
   skeins of red (7107) and three
   skeins of ecru (000)
14-inch square of 10-count
   needlepoint canvas
⅞ yard of dark green fabric
13-inch square of dark red fabric
Polyester fiberfill
1 yard of ⅛-inch-diameter cotton
   piping
Sewing thread
Red laundry marker; brown paper

INSTRUCTIONS

MONOGRAM STITCHERY: En-
large the monogram desired, *opposite,* and transfer the design onto
brown paper. Mark a heavy outline
around the pattern monogram with
the laundry marker.

Draw a 12-inch square on the needlepoint canvas. Center the monogram inside the square under the
canvas; trace the monogram with
the marker. Using a single ply of red
yarn and continental stitches, stitch
monogram. Stitch around the monogram with a single ply of ecru yarn.

PILLOW ASSEMBLY: From green
fabric, cut three 6x36-inch ruffle
strips and a 13-inch square pillow
back. Also from green fabric, cut
and piece ¾-inch-wide bias strips
to cover piping. From red fabric, cut
a 13-inch square pillow front.

Cover piping with bias strips of
green fabric. Sew piping along right
sides of stitched pillow top, matching raw edges. Center and baste the
stitched square to the pillow front;
topstitch just inside piping.

For the ruffle, sew green strips together end to end with right sides
facing; press in half lengthwise with
wrong sides together. Gather raw
edges of ruffle to fit pillow perimeter. Matching raw edges, sew ruffle
to pillow front. With right sides facing, sew pillow back to pillow front
leaving an opening for turning. Trim;
turn and stuff; sew opening closed.

Midnight Sampler

Shown on page 139.
Design is 119 stitches wide and
71 stitches high.
Stitchery is 10¾x6½ inches.

MATERIALS

14x20-inch piece of ecru 11-count
   Aida cloth
Bates Anchor embroidery floss:
   One skein *each* of medium
   brown (375), peach (778),
   medium teal (779), pale teal
   (847), pale pine green (875), dark
   pine green (879), dark rose (897),
   and harvest gold (945)
Graph paper; colored pencils
Embroidery hoop; tapestry needle

INSTRUCTIONS

Referring to the chart on page 146,
transfer the pattern to graph paper
with colored pencils. Or, stitch directly from the page, if desired.

Mark centerlines of the chart.
Baste lines along the centers of Aida
cloth and bind edges with masking
tape or sew small hem.

Stitch design, using centerlines as
points of reference. Use two plies of
floss and work the cross-stitches
over one thread of Aida cloth. Outline angels and hearts with dark
rose backstitches. Stitch the angels'
eyes with French knots using medium brown.

Steam-press the stitchery on the
wrong side and frame as desired.

Twig Jewelry

Shown on page 139.

MATERIALS

¼-inch-thick *dry* slices of a 1½-
   inch-diameter tree branch
Jewelry findings: pin back, earring
   backs, ⅜-inch-diameter spacer
   beads, necklace closure, and
   gold metallic cord
Drill; 1/16-inch drill bit
Liquid plastic
Epoxy glue
Sandpaper
Wallpaper scraps

INSTRUCTIONS

Following manufacturer's instructions, pour liquid plastic over twig
slices; let dry for three days. Sand
edges and paste wallpaper on backs
of slices.

For the necklace, drill holes
through sides of twig slices; thread
the slices onto gold cord, inserting
beads between slices. Fasten the
cording to the necklace closure.

For pins or earrings, glue pin or
earring backs to back of twig slices
with epoxy.

Child's Pinafore

Shown on page 140.
Pinafore fits girls' sizes 6–8.

MATERIALS

Note: Yardages are for 45-inch-
   wide fabrics
¾ yard of red print fabric for
   ruffles, yoke, and pockets
1⅓ yards of red pindot fabric for
   skirt, yoke lining, and neck
   binding
1¼ yards *each* of 2-inch-wide
   single-fold bias tape and ¼-
   inch-wide ecru lace
Scraps of cream pindot (tulip) and
   of green fabric (leaf)
1 yard of purchased green piping
Two ½-inch-diameter green
   buttons
One 5x7-inch piece of fleece
½ yard of ¼-inch-wide green satin
   ribbon

INSTRUCTIONS

Note: Pinafore patterns and measurements include ⅝-inch seam allowances unless otherwise noted.
Tulip pattern includes ¼-inch seam
allowances. Sew seams with right
sides of the fabric facing. Clip all
curved seam allowances and press
seams open.

Cutting instructions
PINAFORE: Enlarge the patterns on
page 147; cut out. Pin the patterns to
the appropriate fabrics (see materials list) and cut out. In addition, cut
continued

MONOGRAMMED PILLOW AND STOCKING

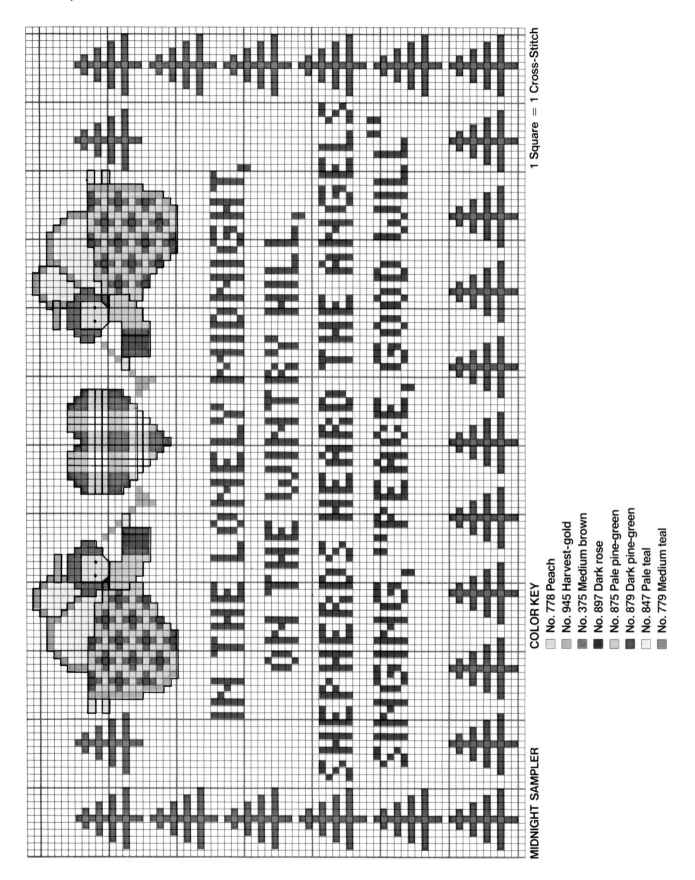

1 Square = 1 Cross-Stitch

COLOR KEY

No. 778 Peach
No. 945 Harvest-gold
No. 375 Medium brown
No. 897 Dark rose
No. 875 Pale pine-green
No. 879 Dark pine-green
No. 847 Pale teal
No. 779 Medium teal

MIDNIGHT SAMPLER

IN THE LONELY MIDNIGHT,
ON THE WINTRY HILL,
SHEPHERDS HEARD THE ANGELS
SINGING, "PEACE, GOOD WILL."

the following: One 22x23-inch skirt front and two 12x23-inch skirt backs, placing the 23-inch sides on the straight of fabric grain. Cut three 4½x32-inch strips for the skirt ruffle.

TULIP DECORATION: Trace the full-size tulip and leaf patterns on page 148 onto tissue paper; cut out. Pin pieces to appropriate fabrics (see materials list); cut out.

Assembly

YOKE: Sew yoke fronts to yoke backs at shoulders. Repeat for lining. Stitch green piping to the bottom edges of the yokes and around the neck edge.

With wrong sides facing, fold the armhole ruffles in half lengthwise; add the lace trim along the folded edges. Mark center of sleeve ruffles along raw edges. Run gathering stitches along raw edges and gather ruffles to fit armhole edges; baste in place matching marked centers at shoulder seams. Press lower edges of yoke lining ⅝ inch to wrong side. Trim to ¼ inch. With right sides facing, sew yoke lining to yoke along armholes and back openings; turn and press.

POCKETS: Trim pockets 2 inches from tops with strips of lace-edged bias tape. Turn under top raw edges ¼ inch; stitch. Turn top to right side along hemline; stitch around pocket ⅝ inch from edge. Turn hem to inside; press. Press under pocket sides and bottom along stitched lines. Sew pockets to pinafore front placing bottom edges 10½ inches from bottom raw edge of skirt.

SKIRT: Sew skirt front to backs at sides, stopping 7 inches from top on each side. Press under seams above stitching. Turn under raw edges ¼ inch; stitch. Topstitch opening ¼ inch from edge.

Sew skirt ruffle pieces end to end to form one long strip. Turn under ¼ inch twice along one long edge to make a hem; stitch. Gather the remaining long edge; join ruffle to the skirt bottom. Turn under ¼ inch

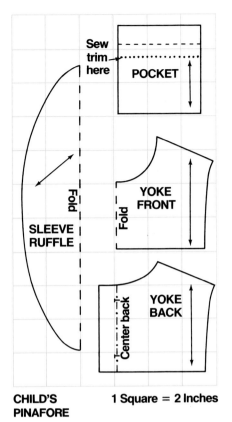

CHILD'S PINAFORE 1 Square = 2 Inches

twice along center back of pinafore skirt edges; stitch in place.

Gather the top edge of the skirt. Sew skirt to yoke, keeping lining edges free. Whipstitch the lining over the seam line.

Trim neck seam allowance to ¼ inch. Cut a bias strip 1x16½ inches. Pin bias strip to neck edge extending strip ends ½ inch beyond back edges. Stitch, using a ¼-inch seam allowance. Turn bias to inside; fold under raw edges and whipstitch to seam line. Make buttonholes in left back; sew on buttons.

TULIP: Lay flower pieces together and leaf pieces together, right sides facing; place fleece on top. Sew layers together leaving marked openings unstitched. Clip tulip points. Turn; stitch openings closed. Referring to photo on page 140, stitch leaf to yoke front following stitching line shown on leaf pattern. Pin tulip to leaf; following the stitching lines shown on tulip pattern, stitch through all thicknesses. Tie ¼-inch ribbon into bow and tack to leaf.

Child's Vest

Shown on page 140.
Vest fits girls' sizes 4–6.

MATERIALS
Note: Yardages are for 45-inch-wide fabrics
1⅛ yards of cream tulip/pindot fabric (upper and lower front, upper back, ruffles, ties, placket, binding)
¼ yard of red pindot fabric (tulip insert, pieced bands)
⅛ yard *each* of two additional coordinating print fabrics (pieced bands)
Green, solid cream, and cream pindot fabric scraps (tulip insert)
1¼ yards *each* of ¾-inch-wide ecru eyelet beading and ¼-inch-wide red ribbon
½ yard of ⅛-inch-wide ribbon
1 yard of piping to coordinate with fabrics
13x22-inch piece of fleece
⅜-inch-diameter ecru button
Sewing thread; ecru quilting thread
Dressmaker's carbon
Tracing wheel

INSTRUCTIONS
Note: The patchwork pieces of the vest are stitched onto a fleece front and back as you assemble these pieces together.

Cutting instructions
TULIP INSERT: Refer to page 148 for the full-size patterns (pieces A–F) to make the templates for the tulip insert. Add ¼-inch seam allowances to all sides of patterns and cut templates from cardboard or plastic. *Note:* When cutting pieces from fabric, cut long side of B and C on the bias; cut long side of F on the straight grain.

Draw around the templates on the wrong sides of the fabrics to mark the pieces. From cream, cut two C pieces, two D pieces, and two F pieces. From green, cut six B pieces. From red pindot fabric, cut two A pieces and four B pieces. From cream pindot, cut one E piece.

continued

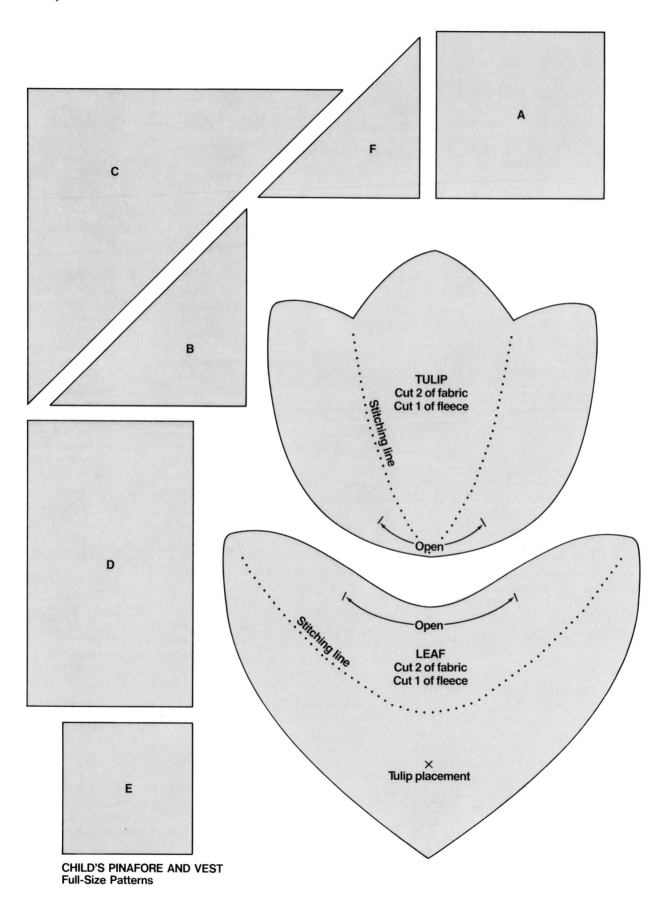

A

F

C

B

TULIP
Cut 2 of fabric
Cut 1 of fleece

Stitching line

Open

D

Open

Stitching line

LEAF
Cut 2 of fabric
Cut 1 of fleece

E

×
Tulip placement

CHILD'S PINAFORE AND VEST
Full-Size Patterns

VEST: Enlarge the patterns, *right.* From cream pindot with tulips, cut upper front, lower front, upper back, full back (lining), full front (lining), and ruffles. In addition, cut the following: Four 3x20-inch ties, one 1¼x10-inch neck placket, and one 2x16½-inch neck bias strip. From fleece, cut complete back and front pieces; transfer markings to fleece pieces with dressmaker's carbon.

TULIP INSERT ASSEMBLY: The insert is assembled into two rectangles, which are then sewed together to complete the insert. Refer to the Child's Vest Insert assembly diagram, *right,* to make the insert block as follows: To begin, sew F triangles to the E square to make a triangle; add the red B triangles to make a small rectangle. Sew the two A squares together; sew long edge of the A's to long edge of Bs to make a square. Sew long sides of D rectangles to opposite sides of the square to complete the top rectangle.

For the bottom half, join long edges of a green B and a red B to form a square. Repeat for a second square. Sew a green B triangle to *each* green side of the two squares to make two triangles. Join triangles along a short side to make a larger triangle. Sew two cream C triangles to the short sides of the large triangle to complete the rectangle.

Join top and bottom rectangles together to complete the insert block.

VEST ASSEMBLY: *Note:* Vest patterns include ¼-inch seam allowances unless otherwise noted. Sew all seams with right sides of fabric facing.

For vest front, baste the tulip insert to the fleece front piece as indicated by the pattern markings. From red pindot, cut two 2x5½-inch and two 2x8½-inch strips. Stitch shorter strips to the insert top and bottom edges through all thicknesses; press strips lightly with a cool iron.

Sew the long strips to the insert side edges; press, checking that the borders lie along the placement lines marked on the fleece.

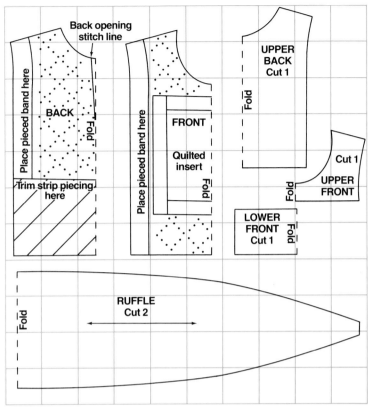

CHILD'S VEST   1 Square = 2 Inches

Cut two 6⅝-inch strips of eyelet beading; thread beading with ¼-inch-wide ribbon. Baste the beading to the top and bottom of the pieced block, with the wrong side of the eyelet facing the right side of the fabric. Repeat using 7⅝-inch-long beading strips for the sides, extending the beading ends ½ inch on each end. Fold under the extensions to miter the corners; tack in place.

Sew the vest upper and lower fronts to the pieced block, stitching through all layers; press. Baste the neck, shoulder, and lower edges to the fleece.

For the back, strip-piece the lower vest by cutting scraps of coordinating fabrics into 1½-inch-wide strips. Cut a 2x2x2½-inch fabric triangle. Stitch the triangle to the center bottom of the fleece back. Using ¼-inch seams, and continuing to sew the strips to the fleece, sew a strip to the opposite side and repeat the procedure until the lower back section of the fleece is filled. Trim the strips even with the trimming line, and the side and bottom edges.

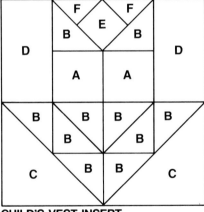

CHILD'S VEST INSERT

Cut a 9¼-inch-long eyelet beading strip; thread beading with ribbon. Baste eyelet to the top edge of the strip-quilted piece with wrong side of the eyelet facing the right side of the fabric.

Sew upper back to lower back (the strip-quilted piece) through all thicknesses; press seams toward the
continued

top neck and shoulder edges to the fleece. Sew the front to the back at the shoulders. Sew piping to front and back bottom edges.

For pieced bands, cut forty 1½-inch squares from coordinating fabrics. Make two strips of 20 squares each, alternating fabrics. Pin each band to the vest, matching the raw edges to the marked placement lines on the fleece. Turn each band under ¼ inch where it meets the strip quilting and slip-stitch the bands to the lower vest. Baste the band side edges to the fleece.

For ties, fold each tie strip in half lengthwise; stitch along the long edge and taper to a point at one end. Turn each tie right side out.

Baste ties, raw edges even, to the lower sides of the front and back above the piping.

For ruffles, fold the ruffle pieces in half lengthwise with wrong sides facing. Gather the long edges and sew the ruffles to the vest sides between the ties.

FINISHING: Stitch the front lining to the two back linings at the shoulders. Sew the lining to the vest along the side and bottom edges. Turn the vest right side out through the neck opening; press.

Stitch the back opening sewing line; slash between the stitching. Baste piping to the neck edge. For the button loop, double-fold a ¾x2-inch fabric strip; edge-stitch. Baste the loop to the right neck edge below the piping.

Sew the placket to the back opening; press seam toward the placket. Turn the placket to the outside. Fold under ¼ inch on the raw edge and stitch. Turn the right back placket to the inside.

Pin the neck bias strip to the neck extending the strips ends ½ inch beyond the back edges; stitch. Turn the bias to the inside; fold under the raw edges and whipstitch to the seam line. Sew on the neck button.

Hand-quilt along the quilting lines indicated on the patterns on page 149. Quilt the patchwork tulip as desired; attach a ribbon bow at bottom of tulip.

Rag Doll

Shown on page 140.

MATERIALS
¼ yard of peach fabric (body, arms)
8x16-inch piece of black fabric (legs)
¼ yard *each* of red print fabric (dress) and green print fabric (apron)
9x20-inch piece of white fabric (pantaloon)
58 yards of tan two-ply yarn (hair)
DMC embroidery floss: one skein *each* of pink (604) and black (310)
½ pound of polyester fiberfill
Pale pink marker
20 inches of ¼-inch-wide elastic
12 inches of ⅜-inch-wide green ribbon
Sewing thread
Two snaps
Tracing paper

INSTRUCTIONS
Note: All patterns and measurements include ¼-inch seam allowances. Sew seams with right sides of the fabrics facing. Clip curved seam allowances and press seams open where possible.

Trace the full-size patterns, *opposite* and on page 152, onto tracing paper; cut out. Cut pieces from fabrics as listed in materials list. In addition, cut one 7x27-inch red-print dress skirt, two 5x9-inch red-print sleeves, and one 6¼x26-inch green-print apron skirt.

ARMS AND LEGS: For each limb, sew units together, with right sides facing, leaving tops and openings between Xs unstitched.

Turn arms and legs to right sides; stitch across the joint lines as indicated on patterns.

BODY: With right sides facing, tuck arm and leg ends to fit between the dots on one head/body piece. Baste in place with raw edges even.

Pin remaining head/body piece over the first, enclosing the arms and legs. Stitch, leaving an opening for turning on one side. Turn and stuff body, arms, and legs; sew all openings closed.

FACE: Transfer facial features to one face circle. Satin-stitch the pupils and backstitch the remaining lines, using three plies of black floss. Color cheeks with marker. With right sides facing, sew face circles together leaving an opening for turning; clip curves. Turn and stuff lightly; sew opening closed. Pin the face over the head/body piece, matching edges. Whipstitch all around.

HAIR: Wrap yarn around an 8-inch piece of cardboard 65 times; cut one end; remove cardboard. Spread the yarn bunch to about 3 inches wide; machine-stitch through the center. Repeat to make another hair shank. Tack one bunch to the top of the head with the stitched line running parallel to and ⅛ inch in front of the seam connecting the head pieces. Trim yarn in front for bangs. Tack second hair bunch perpendicular to the first (stitched line running from the base of the bangs to the back of the head). Trim and style hair.

DRESS: Sew bodice front to bodice backs at shoulders. Gather one long edge of each sleeve and sew to bodice sleeve edges. Turn under ¼ inch twice on sleeve ends for hems; stitch. Zigzag-stitch a 2-inch length of elastic 1 inch from each sleeve hem for ruffle. Sew underarm/side seams. Bind the neck edge with a green bias strip.

Gather one long edge of skirt piece; stitch to bodice waist. Sew center back seam to 1 inch below the bodice. Turn under ¼ inch twice along the back openings; stitch. Attach snaps at neck and waist. Hem.

PANTALOON: Sew the center front crotch seam. Turn under top edge and zigzag-stitch a 7-inch length of elastic along inside edge, pulling elastic taut to gather waist.

continued

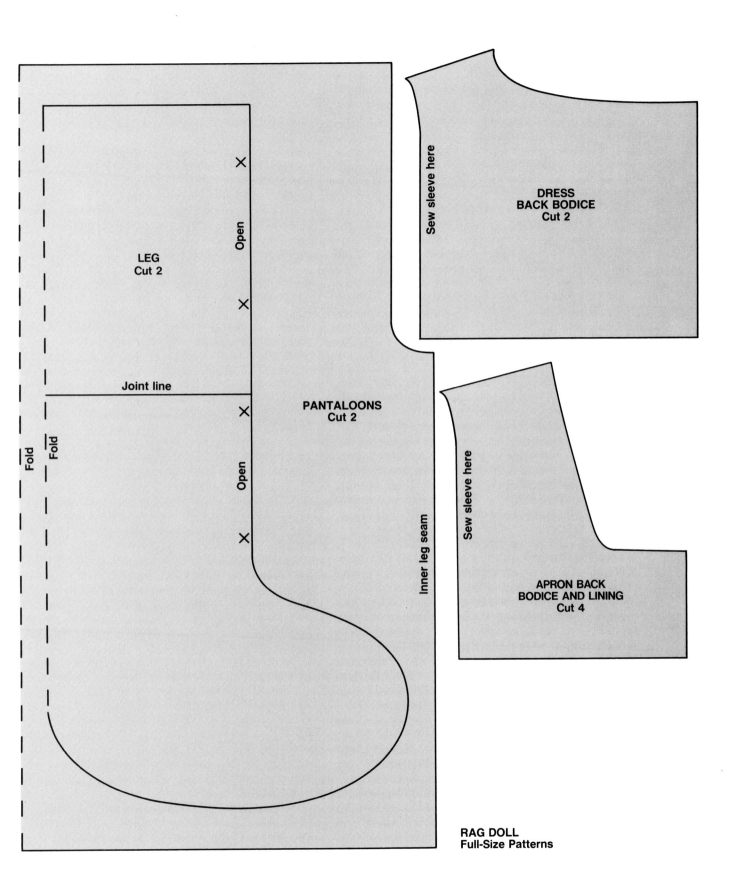

LEG
Cut 2

Open

Joint line

Fold

Fold

Open

PANTALOONS
Cut 2

Inner leg seam

DRESS
BACK BODICE
Cut 2

Sew sleeve here

APRON BACK
BODICE AND LINING
Cut 4

Sew sleeve here

RAG DOLL
Full-Size Patterns

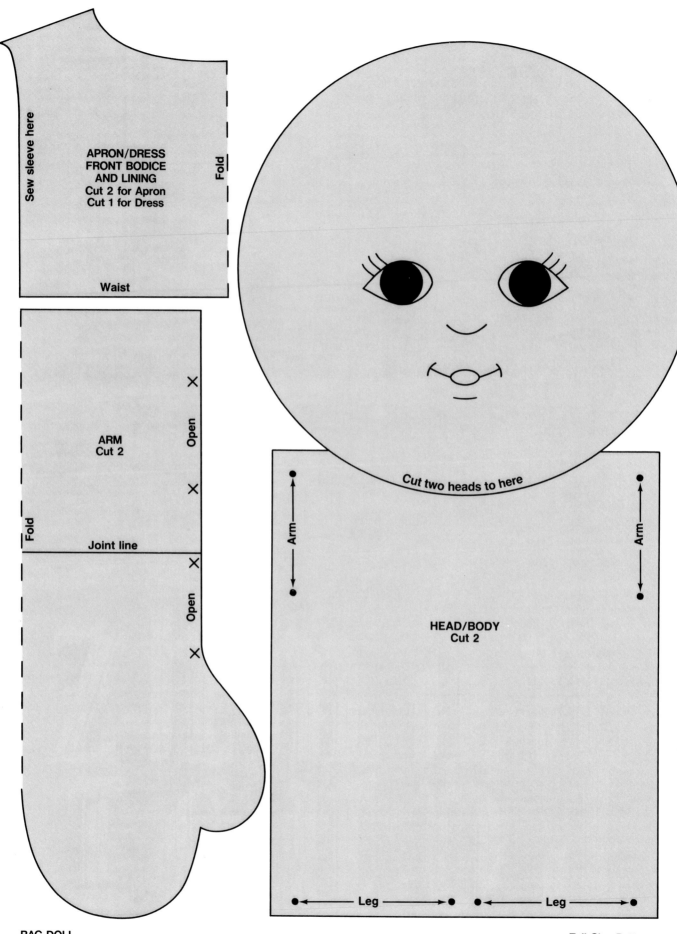

APRON/DRESS
FRONT BODICE
AND LINING
Cut 2 for Apron
Cut 1 for Dress

Sew sleeve here

Fold

Waist

ARM
Cut 2

Fold

Open

Open

Joint line

Cut two heads to here

Arm

Arm

HEAD/BODY
Cut 2

Leg

Leg

RAG DOLL

152

Turn fabric under ¼ inch twice along each leg bottom for a hem; stitch. Zigzag-stitch over a 4½-inch length of elastic 1 inch from each hem, pulling elastic taut to gather leg ruffle. Sew center back crotch and inner leg seams.

APRON: Sew bodice backs to bodice front at shoulders. Repeat for lining. Cut the ⅜-inch-wide ribbon in half. Tack a ribbon half to the center of each side of bodice back, raw edges even. Tuck ribbons in and sew lining to bodice around side, back, and neck edges. Turn and press. Turn under ¼ inch twice on apron skirt bottom for the hem; stitch. Turn under ¼ inch twice on center back edges of apron bodice.

Gather top of apron skirt to fit apron bodice waist; stitch skirt to the bodice.

Dog and Cat Puzzles

Shown on page 141.

MATERIALS
Two 1¼x9x12-inch pine boards
Woodburning tool
Sandpaper
Carbon paper
Clear polyurethane varnish

INSTRUCTIONS
Enlarge the dog and cat puzzle patterns, *right;* transfer the patterns onto pine boards with carbon paper. Woodburn the facial details (noses, mouths, and eyes) following the dotted lines on the patterns.

With band saw, cut out puzzle pieces along solid lines. Sand all edges. Seal all surfaces with two coats of clear polyurethane varnish, sanding lightly between coats.

Reindeer Toy

Shown on page 141.

MATERIALS
⅓ yard *each* of light brown and white fake fur fabric
Black velveteen scrap (nose)
Brown, black, and white felt scraps (eyes)
Black crewel yarn; sewing thread
White carpet thread
Curved needle
Fourteen 12-inch pipe cleaners
White fabric paint
½ pound of polyester fiberfill
Unger Roly-Sport yarn (50-gram ball): one ball *each* of red (4864) and green (4876)
Size 5 knitting needles
Graph paper

INSTRUCTIONS
Note: All patterns include ¼-inch seam allowances. Sew seams with right sides of fabric facing unless otherwise indicated.

Enlarge the reindeer pattern on page 154 onto graph paper; cut out pattern pieces.

From light brown fur, cut two body tops, one tail, two ears, and two heads. From white fur, cut one body bottom, one tail, two ears, and one front facing.

BODY AND HEAD: Sew the two body tops together along the center seam line.

Sew the two tails together, leaving straight edge unstitched; turn right side out. Center the tail with the white side down and raw edges even; stitch in place on the body top. Re-stitch the center seam, extending it to enclose the tail.

Sew the heads together along the center seam line between the dots. Stitch the head to the body top, matching center seams.

Sew the front facing to the body bottom at the neck edges. Sew the body top to the body bottom, leaving the marked opening unstitched. Turn the body right side out.

For leg supports, twist seven pipe cleaners together, forming two 15-inch lengths. Insert each end of one pipe cleaner twist into a hind leg

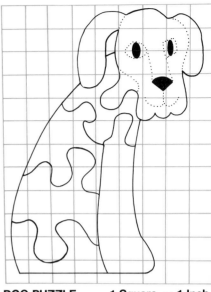

DOG PUZZLE   **1 Square = 1 Inch**

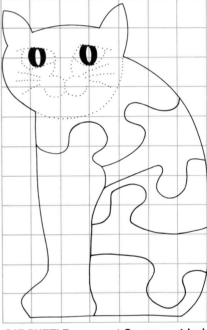

CAT PUZZLE   **1 Square = 1 Inch**

with the center of the twist spanning the body. Repeat for forelegs. Stuff the body; sew opening closed.

EARS: Sew the brown and white ear pieces together in pairs, leaving openings for turning; turn and slip-stitch openings closed. Gather bottoms of ears. Using curved needle, stitch ears to head with white sides facing forward.

continued

FACE: Cut the nose from black velveteen. Cut two black felt eyelashes, two white felt eyes, and two brown pupils.

Gather the edge of the nose; stuff; sew to the head. Glue the eyelashes behind the top of the white felt eyes; add white carpet thread highlights to pupils with three satin stitches and glue the pupils to the eyes. Stitch the eyes to the head with sewing thread. Referring to the photo on page 141, straight-stitch the reindeer's mouth with two plies of black crewel yarn.

SCARF: With green yarn, cast on 15 stitches. Work in garter stitch (knit every row) for 1¾ inches. Change to red yarn and work for 1¾ inches more; change back to green. Continue in this manner, making red and green stripes, until scarf has seven green blocks. Bind off loosely and weave in yarn ends.

FINISHING: Dot white fabric paint spots over the back and sides of the body. Tie knitted scarf around the reindeer's neck.

Fox Toy

Shown on page 141.

MATERIALS

½ yard *each* of light brown and white fake fur fabric
Black velveteen scrap (nose)
Black crewel yarn
Curved needle
Sewing thread; carpet thread
Graph paper; polyester fiberfill

INSTRUCTIONS

Note: Patterns include ¼-inch seam allowances. Sew seams with right sides of fabrics facing unless otherwise directed.

Enlarge the pattern for the fox toy, *right,* onto graph paper; cut out pattern pieces.

From light brown fur, cut two *each* of ear, tail, head side, head top, and body top pieces. From white fur, cut two ears, two tail tips, and one *each* of head bottom, muzzle, and body bottom.

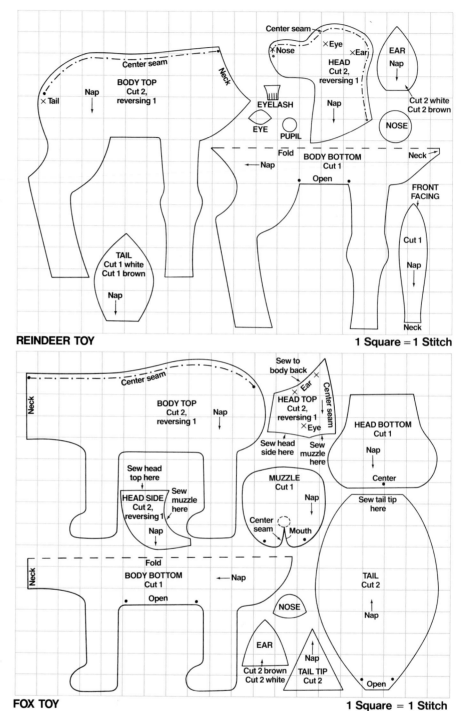

REINDEER TOY 1 Square = 1 Stitch

FOX TOY 1 Square = 1 Stitch

HEAD: Sew the head tops together at the center seam. Sew the head side pieces to the head top. Stitch muzzle center seam to the matching dots; sew muzzle to the pieced head.

Sew one brown and one white ear piece together, leaving an opening at the bottom for turning. Repeat with the other ear pieces. Turn the

ears right side out; slip-stitch the openings closed. Using the curved needle, sew the ears to each side of the head with the white fabric sides facing forward.

Join the pieced head to the head bottom, matching the muzzle seam to the head bottom center. Turn right side out.

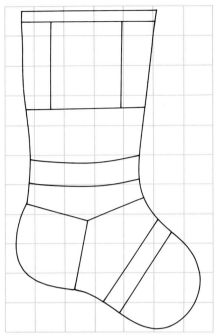

MONOGRAMMED STOCKING
1 Square = 2 Inches

BODY: Sew the body top center seam. Sew the body top to the body bottom, leaving the marked opening and the neck unstitched.

With the right sides facing, join the head to the body at the neck.

Turn the fox right side out; stuff; sew the opening closed.

TAIL: Sew a white tail tip to each light brown tail. Sew the tail pieces together, leaving the marked opening unstitched. Turn right side out, stuff, and sew opening closed. Sew the tail to the body using carpet thread and a curved needle. Stitch twice through all thicknesses.

FACE: Cut the nose from velveteen. Gather the edges; stuff.

Sew nose to the muzzle. Straight-stitch eyes and a mouth with three plies of black crewel yarn following the markings on the pattern for placement of each feature.

Monogrammed Stocking

Shown on page 142.
Finished stocking is 21½ inches long.

MATERIALS

½ yard of green print fabric
Five ⅛-yard lengths *each* of five red-and-green print fabrics
15x22-inch piece of fleece
DMC Floralia 3-ply Persian wool yarn: One skein of ecru and two skeins of red (7107)
8-inch square of 10-count needlepoint canvas
Permanent marker
Graph paper
Red sewing thread

INSTRUCTIONS

Note: Sew all seams with right sides facing. Add ½-inch seam allowances to each pattern piece before cutting from fabric.

Enlarge the stocking pattern, *left*, onto graph paper. Cut one entire stocking *each* from fleece and green print fabric. Cut patchwork pieces for the stocking front from red fabrics. In addition, cut two 2¾x10½-inch rectangles from the dark green print for stocking top facings. Transfer the patchwork placement lines on pattern to fleece stocking shape.

MONOGRAM: Enlarge the monogram pattern of your choice onto graph paper using the patterns on page 145. Mark a 4¾x5½-inch block in the center of the needlepoint canvas. Center the enlarged monogram pattern under the square and trace it onto the canvas with a permanent marker. Using 3 plies of ecru yarn, stitch the monogram with basket-weave stitch. Fill in the background with red yarn. Trim the canvas, leaving ½-inch seam allowances around the worked needlepoint.

STOCKING FRONT: Place the toe patch right side up on the fleece, matching raw edges (refer to the pattern for placement). Stitch along the straight line through both layers.

With right sides facing, sew the adjoining patchwork strip to the toe piece along the same line; open and press to the right side. Join the remaining patchwork pieces and the needlepoint monogram in the same manner.

STOCKING ASSEMBLY: Sew one long edge of a facing rectangle to the top edge of the stocking front; press open to the right side. Repeat for the stocking back.

Lay two strands of red tapestry yarn over each patchwork seam; with a loose machine-zigzag stitch, sew over the yarn, couching it to the stocking front.

Sew the stocking front to the back; turn right side out. Turn the facing raw edge under ½ inch and stitch. Fold the facing to the inside; tack in place.

Calico Dolls

Shown on pages 142 and 143.
Finished doll is 8¾ inches tall.

MATERIALS
For each doll

⅓ yard *each* of two coordinating print fabrics (body, skirt)
Scrap of off-white single-knit fabric (head, hands)
Scrap of DMC black pearl cotton, size 5 (eyes)
Two skeins of DMC pearl cotton, size 5, in desired color for hair
Two ⅜-inch heart-shaped buttons
Carpet thread to match buttons
18 inches of ⅜-inch-wide ribbon in color to complement fabrics (sash)
Sewing thread in black (eyes), pink (mouth), and colors to match fabrics
Tracing paper
Powdered blush
Dressmaker's carbon paper
Polyester fiberfill
Soft-sculpture needle
Four ⅛-inch-diameter beads (buttons)
Lace trims and accessories as desired

continued

INSTRUCTIONS

Note: Sew seams with right sides facing unless otherwise noted.

Trace the full-size patterns, *right,* onto tracing paper. Add a ¼-inch seam allowance to each piece and cut out.

Cut body and base from one print fabric; cut a 10½x24-inch skirt rectangle from another print fabric. Cut head circles from knit fabric.

For arms, prepare fabrics by joining the long edges of a 3½x5-inch print fabric rectangle (fabric to match body fabric) and a 1½x5-inch knit fabric rectangle. Cut the arms from the pieced square, placing the hand on the knit fabric with the seam at the wrist.

HEAD: Transfer facial details to one head piece using carbon paper. On the same head piece, use black pearl cotton to make French knot eyes. Straight-stitch eyelashes and under-eye lines with black sewing thread.

Embroider the mouth with a double strand of pink floss using an outline stitch for the curve, French knots for the corners, and straight stitches for the center lines. Make cheeks rosy with blush.

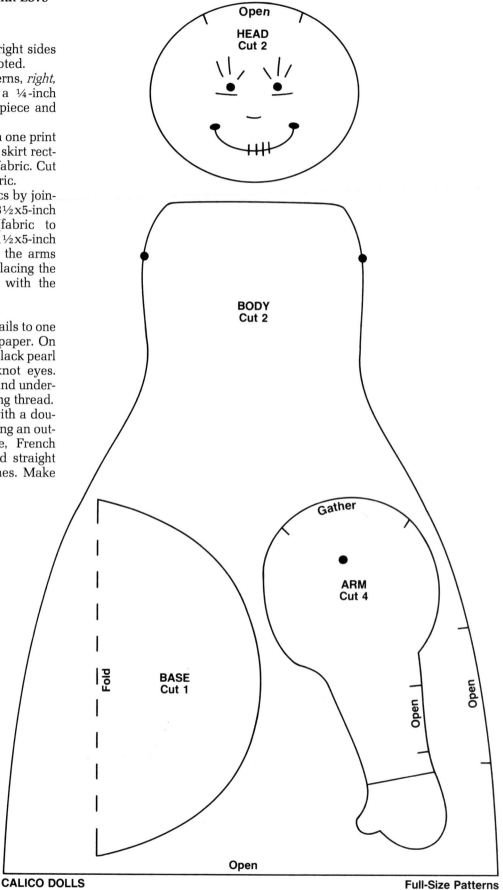

CALICO DOLLS

Full-Size Patterns

Sew head front to head back leaving the marked opening unstitched. Turn right side out, stuff, and sew the opening closed.

HAIR: Untwist two skeins of pearl cotton. Lay the skeins side by side lengthwise; spread them to a 2-inch width. Sew through the center of the skeins to form a stitched part. Center the part on the doll's head; tack in place. Style doll's hair as desired.

BODY: Sew body front to back leaving marked opening unstitched. Sew base to body bottom.

Turn body right side out; stuff with fiberfill and sew the opening closed. Hand-sew head to body.

ARMS: Sew the arms together in pairs leaving the marked openings unstitched. Gather the top of each arm along the stitched seams with a short running stitch. Stuff the arms; sew the openings closed.

Thread soft-sculpture needle with a doubled length of carpet thread. Push the needle through the body from the left side to the right side at dots indicated on the pattern. Poke the needle through the right arm, through one heart button, then back through button and arm; knot thread under arm to fasten.

Attach left arm as for right.

SKIRT: Join the short edges of the skirt rectangle forming a tube. Fold the tube in half lengthwise with the wrong sides facing. Gather the raw edges on one long side to fit the doll's waist; hand-sew to doll.

FINISHING: Tie a ⅜-inch ribbon sash around the waist to conceal the skirt raw edges or create an apron by gathering a hemmed 5x12-inch rectangle onto a ribbon waistband. Sew bead buttons to bodice and accessorize as desired.

SAFETY TIPS FOR A HAPPY HOLIDAY SEASON

As enchanting as it is, your family's beautiful evergreen with its twinkling lights and glittering decorations can be a safety hazard. Take these precautions to guard against fire and other accidents in your home during the holiday season.

CHOOSING A TREE: If you buy an artificial Christmas tree, make sure it's been tested for flammability by Underwriters Laboratories and bears their seal of approval.

If you opt for a real tree, choose a fresh one. Fresh trees have a high moisture content. They are less likely to dry out and catch fire. If the needles are brown and break off easily, the tree is a greater fire risk.

Test the needles by flexing them between your thumb and forefinger. The needles should bend but not break. Next, lift the tree a few inches off the ground, then drop it on its base. Only a few needles should fall.

Store a fresh tree outdoors or in your garage in a bucket of water, away from the sun and wind, until you're ready to bring it indoors and decorate it. Mist the tree occasionally to keep the branches moist.

SETTING UP A TREE: Just before you bring the tree inside, cut an inch or two off the bottom of the trunk so the tree can take in water easily.

Clean the tree stand with a small amount of household bleach mixed with water before you use it.

Place the tree in a location away from fireplaces, radiators, and other heat sources. Avoid placing the tree where it interferes with the traffic pattern in your home.

All through the holiday season, keep the tree moist. Fill the tree stand with enough lukewarm water to cover the cut end of the trunk, and keep it at that level. Check the amount of water in the stand daily; refill the stand as necessary so the trunk end is always covered with water.

DECORATING A TREE: **Never use lighted candles on a tree or near evergreens or draperies.** Instead, use electric lights that have been approved for safety. (Look for the Underwriters Laboratories seal.)

Check each light set for broken or cracked sockets, frayed or bare wires, and loose connections. Repair or discard faulty light strings.

Replace any burned-out lamps on electrical decorations only with the lamps specified on the package.

Use only the manufacturer's specified fuses to replace burned-out fuses on light strings. Never use aluminum foil or fuses with different ratings to replace burned-out fuses. As you fasten lights to the tree, avoid letting the bulbs touch the needles or branches.

Credits

We would like to express our gratitude and appreciation to the many people who helped with this book.

Our heartfelt thanks go to each of the artists and designers, who so enthusiastically contributed ideas, designs, and projects.

Thanks also to the photographers, whose creative talents and technical skills added much to the book.

We are happy as well to acknowledge our indebtedness to the companies, collectors, needlecrafters, and others who generously shared their stitched pieces and projects with us, or in some other way contributed to the production of this book.

Designers

Amy Albert—140, doll
Linda Beardsley—14, mitten ornaments; 54, serape stockings; 58, 60, bird ornament
Barb Bergman—14, heart ornaments; 62, bird stitchery
Teresa Boernke—13, doll; 122–123
Gary Boling—11, monogram pillow; 99, heart adaptation; 100–101, wooden heart cutouts, carved pine hearts, and wheat bundle ornaments; 102, painted hearts; 124, painted tin stars

Susan Carson—54–55, angel dolls; 58–59, rag ball and angel ornaments
Coats and Clark—76, afghan
Laurie Craven—98, sampler; 105; 126–127
Phyllis Dunstan—36; 38, cotton Santa; 142–143, dolls

Linda Emmerson—103
Chris Evenson—101, hardanger ornaments
Dixie Falls—9; 32–33; 116–117
Karen Flanscha—100, shadow-quilted ornaments
Jaclyn Garlock—38, chimney Santa
Lee Gatzke—142, stocking
Connie Jo Godwin—125
Sandi Guely—138, pillow

Naomi Hart—141, stuffed toys
Jan Hawks—54, strip-pieced patchwork quilt
Barbara Hickey—12, bear pull toy
Ingleman Designs—140, pinafore and vest
Rebecca Jerdee—139, twig jewelry; 141, puzzles
Marjorie Wedge Mable—37
Dana McDill—74, toy boat
Nancy Antisdel Nielsen—104
Chris Noah-Cooper—8, paper dove
Patty Reed—12, dolls
Ruth Reetz—81

Margaret Sindelar—6, peppermint wreaths; 15, stocking; 63, patchwork pillows; 74, stocking
Lorie Skahen—10
Barbara Smith—56
Diana Smith—39
Ciba Vaughan—14, glove ornaments
Sue Veigulis—78–79, awning stripe ornaments
Lois Watson—139, sampler
Bonnie Wedge—94–95

Jim Williams—6, alphabet ornaments; 6, velvet roses; 8, gilt walnuts; 11, alphabet sampler and holly pillow; 54, necklaces; 57; 58, drum ornaments; 60, wreath and linen wrapped candles; 61, table runner; 62, bird stencil picture; 63, folk art rocking toys; 76–77; 78–79, fish lure ornaments and cardboard stars
Dee Wittmack—90–91

Photographers

Hopkins Associates—32–33; 90–91; 94–95; 138–143
Terry Husebye—54–63
Scott Little—36–39; 116–117
William Stites—74–81
Perry Struse—6–15; 50–51; 98–105; 122–127

Acknowledgments

Aarlan
21 Adley Road
Cambridge, MA 02138

Bernartex, Inc.
1412 Broadway, 11th Floor
New York, NY 10018

Buckboard Antiques and Quilts
Judy Howard
1411 N. May
Oklahoma City, OK 73107

Charles Craft, Inc.
Box 1049
Laurinburg, NC 28352

C.M. Offray and Son, Inc.
261 Madison Ave.
New York, NY 10016

Coats and Clark, Inc.
Dept. CS
P.O. Box 1010
Toccoa, GA 30577

DMC Corporation
197 Trumbull St.
Elizabeth, NJ 07206

Susan Bates, Inc.
212 Middlesex Ave.
Chester, CT 06412

INDEX

For photographs, see pages noted in **bold** type; remaining page numbers refer to how-to instructions.

Have BETTER HOMES AND
GARDENS® magazine delivered to
your door. For information, write to:
ROBERT AUSTIN
P.O. BOX 4536
DES MOINES, IA 50336